Beyond Reason

Beyond Reason

How Miracles Can Change Your Life

PAT ROBERTSON

WITH

WILLIAM PROCTOR

WILLIAM MORROW AND COMPANY, INC.
NEW YORK

Library of Congress Catalog Card Number: 61470

ISBN: 0-688-02214-6

Printed in the United States of America

First Edition

1 2 3 4 5 6 7 8 9 10

BOOK DESIGN BY ROBERT FREESE

Contents

Introduction

In the twentieth century, is there a possibility that God will reach down into the lives of ordinary people to perform extraordinary acts which through the centuries men have termed miracles?

The answer to that question is a resounding Yes! In the last twenty-five years, it has been my privilege to witness thousands of dramatic occurrences for which there was no explanation other than the explanation of faith. They were indeed "beyond reason."

This book is a compilation of a few of these extraordinary happenings, along with guidelines to show how miracles of finance, spiritual protection, and physical healing can take place in this life today.

Beyond Reason

CHAPTER ONE

What Are Miracles and How Can They Change Your Life?

Back in 1977, unusual weather conditions threatened to destroy the orange groves in Norvell Hayes's part of Florida. The trees in the area were covered with icicles, and the orange growers knew from past experience that it was highly likely that the cold would kill their crops.

But Norvell wasn't willing to accept the disaster that seemed inevitable. He believed God could save his trees, and he asked for a miracle.

"I got in my car, drove to the orange grove, and parked along the highway," he said. "I just looked at the grove and told the devil to take his hands off the orange trees. Then I asked the Father, in Jesus' name, to let His power come and hover around my fruit trees and not let them die."

A few weeks later, the sun began to shine again and things warmed up. Norvell still gets excited when he describes the result of his prayer. "Fruit was developing on my trees! The twenty-five hundred orange trees on the property across the road, which was owned by another grower, were dead. But on my side of the road, it was different. It was as though a shield had been placed on my property line, which stopped the potentially damaging frost from crossing it. I didn't lose a tree."

Now, I'll freely admit that a number of years ago, before I became familiar with what you might call the "Miracle Dimension" of reality, I would have been skeptical of a report like this. Yet it's clear that something incredible had happened on Norvell Hayes's property. Our film crew recorded the event, and the evidence is there for any eye to behold. Despite that killer frost, his orange grove is still producing fruit. In my judgment, this incident just can't be adequately explained in terms of an ordinary, "natural" scheme of reality.

Since I entered into a serious, intimate relationship with God through a commitment to Jesus Christ back in 1956, I have encountered tens of thousands of miracles like this. They cover the range of the challenges and problems we face as human beings, including such things as:

- a pilot's survival during an airplane crash that seemed certain to result in death;
- the instantaneous healing of a man whom doctors diagnosed as being hopelessly, terminally ill;
- the complete, immediate release of alcoholics and drug addicts from their destructive habits;
- the injection of love and peace into stormy, hate-filled marriages;

- the diversion of natural disasters like hurricanes from cities that weather forecasters had predicted would be devastated;
- financial provision in ways that are very difficult for the mind to accept.

But by now you may be saying, "Can I ever be sure that such things really happen? And even if they do, is there really any possibility that I can experience them myself?

The answer to both of these questions is yes. But if you're not accustomed to dealing with the marvelous world of miracles, you may understandably be skeptical. So it will be helpful to accord this whole area of reality a further examination.

First of all, it's important to recognize that things are often quite different from the way they first appear. A figure swimming under water may initially seem to be a large, brightly hued fish. But when the "fish" surfaces, a scuba diver wearing flippers and a multicolored bathing suit comes into view. Or a steady beam of light low in the early evening sky may at first seem to be an airplane, with landing lights on, heading down to a local airfield. But on closer inspection, when the "airplane light" fails to move, you realize you are looking at a particularly brilliant appearance of the evening star, the planet Venus.

By the same token, it's easy to be fooled into thinking that all reality is contained in our physical world—in the three-dimensional realm of our five senses. We've been conditioned to believe that hardheaded, rational, no-nonsense people should accept only the natural world as *really* real. If you can touch it, taste it, smell it, see it, or hear it, then you're dealing with something genuine. We are told that you can believe in or comprehend only those persons or things that stand up under rigorous scientific verification. If the laws of chemistry, applied physics, and Aristotelian logic can't be invoked, you shouldn't waste your time.

This view of the universe is based on what philosophers or theoretical scientists might call a closed system of reality. In other words, according to this view, everything that exists is encompassed by the ordinary physical world and the laws that govern it. Conversely, nothing exists that cannot be fully known by human beings through the laws of the natural system.

This is a way of looking at things that has popped up relatively recently, beginning with Isaac Newton's approach to physics in the eighteenth century. The near-worshipful veneration of Newton—even in his own time, in the so-called Age of the Enlightenment—comes through in these lines from his contemporary, Alexander Pope.

> *Nature and Nature's laws lay hid in night:*
> *God said, Let Newton be! and all was light.*

Now, I don't mean to criticize Newton himself because he was certainly a great scientist, one who has contributed immeasurably to our understanding of the physical universe. And he was also a deeply religious man, a devotee of in-depth Bible study who would have been the last to claim that he had opened the way to a complete knowledge of God and the universe.

But many scientists and philosophers who followed Newton were not so humble. They put human reason on a pedestal that left little room at the top for an infinite, unsearchable, dynamic Deity. In a very fundamental sense, then, man and his earthbound abilities became the measure of all things, both secular and religious. God might still exist as a sort of abstract principle. Or perhaps, as the Deists would have it, He continued as a Creator who set the physical world in motion and then sat back and watched it putter along, without intervening in the natural laws He had established.

WHAT ARE MIRACLES?

Clearly, this Enlightenment concept of reality was heading in an entirely different direction from that of the sovereign God of the Universe, who is revealed in the Bible.

But such a perception of reality has problems. In the first place, there are things that simply can't be explained in the scientific framework established centuries ago by Isaac Newton—a framework still employed by "practical" or "applied" scientists in our own day.

For example, ordinary Newtonian physics can't fully explain the nature of light and the limits of its ultimate speed. And today's physicists who are exploring "unified" concepts of subatomic particles and waves must go well beyond Newton's ideas as they build successive new theories.

Well-trained practical scientists may also stumble around as they try to grasp the meaning of the "near-death" or "temporary death" experiences, including visions and out-of-body sensations, which have been discussed in many recent popular books and scientific studies. And the instantaneous healing of a terminal illness, which defies any explanation by laboratory analysis, leaves even the best physicians shaking their heads and muttering, "I just don't know!"

So scientists, engineers, or physicians—and their lay followers and admirers—may understand the nuts and bolts of *applied* physics, chemistry, engineering, or medicine. But they often have no understanding at all of how to deal with extraordinary occurrences. Either they deny the reality of what has happened, or they try to offer limited explanations based on their own narrow fields of training.

Such attempts always fall short, however, and for one major reason: The basic tools and training that applied scientists rely on are inadequate to explain all of reality. Present equipment and practical technological know-how simply won't permit us to measure or understand such mysteries as the overnight disappearance of a deadly cancer, or the beginning of the universe—any more than they'll allow us to quantify the beauty of an exquisite rainbow.

In an effort to fill this vacuum in scientific understanding, a new class of scientist has come to the fore in this century: These are the *theoretical* physicists, astronomers, and other abstract-thinking specialists who have tried to break free of the earthbound, time-limited Newtonian universe.

The late Albert Einstein, of course, was the foremost of these thinkers. His insights, including the theory of relativity, have finally helped us understand things like the constant speed of light. But even as Einstein and his disciples have been parting the curtains ever so slightly on additional mysteries of the universe, an infinity of questions remain to be answered. And increasing numbers of scientists and philosophers are acknowledging that the Enlightenment assumption that man has the capacity to understand all reality is sadly lacking. Indeed, it appears that there are boundaries beyond which our minds will never take us.

Perhaps the most dramatic recent statement of this sense of human limitation came in a recent article in *The New York Times Magazine*. The author, Robert Jastrow, director of NASA's Goddard Institute for Space Studies and a self-described agnostic, wrote:

> At this moment it seems as though science will never be able to raise the curtain on the mystery of Creation. For the scientist who has lived by his faith in the power of reason, the story ends like a bad dream. He has scaled the mountains of ignorance; he is about to conquer the highest peak; as he pulls himself over the final rock, he is

greeted by a band of theologians who have been sitting there for centuries.*

So this is where we find ourselves at the end of the twentieth century. After nearly three hundred years of high-flying faith in the limitless capacity of man's mind, we find that there *are* limits to our brain power. We find that we don't live in a closed system that can be completely understood if smart humans just work hard enough at it. On the contrary, the real universe is open-ended in a frightening sense that we can't begin to comprehend. Things are not at all what they seem. And so we are thrown back on explanations of reality and the universe that, though long discarded or scoffed at by the scientific establishment, are now being taken seriously again.

What we're talking about here is a vast, expansive reality, of which our time-bound physical world occupies only a small niche. This is not in any sense a self-contained system, as Newton thought. Rather, even though the *totality* of what is real includes natural laws and principles, these are often only secondary to more significant supernatural, or "extradimensional," forces.

The late Cambridge University scholar C. S. Lewis described this cosmic state of affairs in his book *Miracles* when he wrote: "In one sense the laws of Nature cover the whole field of space and time; in another, what they leave out is precisely the whole real universe—the incessant torrent of actual events which makes up true history. That must come from somewhere else."

In short, we are confronted with an open-ended flow of world history featuring what have traditionally been called miracles—an arena that is beyond reason.

*"Have Astronomers Found God?" *The New York Times Magazine*, June 25, 1978, p. 29.

But what exactly is a miracle? A miracle might be defined as a concrete breakthrough from the invisible, supernatural world into our own visible, natural world. The result is an event that becomes a part of the flow of our history but has been caused or generated in a supernatural reality outside our own.

The ultimate source of the miracle—the Initiator or Prime Mover, if you will—is the Creator of the Universe whom we call God. God is a person. But His reality goes far beyond what we know as personal and encompasses the broadest cosmic reaches of being.

God created the Universe and dwells above it. As theologians put it, "He is transcendent, but He is free at any time to enter into the affairs of His Universe—including our earth—whenever He chooses. He is therefore with us or 'imminent.'"

It is clear, therefore, that if you hope to understand how miracles work, you have to understand God. You have to believe in His existence and His interest in our lives. And most important, you have to be involved in a personal relationship with Him—a relationship that arises from a firm commitment on your part.

But many people today feel totally self-sufficient. Why change their lives to accommodate a supernatural, invisible God? Why not just make do with the comfortable world that they can see and feel?

One problem is that our physical world is not that predictable. Accidents, disease, or emotional strains often strike us or our loved ones so unexpectedly that our world seems to crumble around us. Then we, and millions like us, desperately wish for some outside, preferably divine, intervention to help us out.

The longer we live, the more we realize that the natural world has little permanence and that the only true reality and stability are found in the invisible world. The world where God dwells. The world of miracles. Sooner or later we realize that

WHAT ARE MIRACLES?

God has provided to those who know Him a world of power that can:

- restore broken and diseased bodies;
- heal mental and emotional problems;
- provide signs or guideposts to help us escape confusion and find the proper direction for our lives;
- rescue us from physical danger;
- lead those separated from God to salvation;
- enlighten those who are ignorant of the potential of the supernatural;
- mend broken marriages;
- increase the faith of those who have already embarked on a personal relationship with God;
- bring happiness to those burdened by the cares of the world;
- exercise dominion over the physical world, including the weather.

The real drama and excitement begin when we consider specific examples of how the visible world can transform our visible but limited earthly existence. You've already met Norvell Hayes, who witnessed the suspension of the laws of nature when his orange grove in Florida was rescued from a killer frost. Countless others have reported miracles that have not only defied all medical and scientific explanations but have also touched our deepest feelings.

My own understanding of miracles—and my personal belief in the extent to which God can intervene in our natural realm—has been a gradual process. In part, my faith has grown because of the thousands upon thousands of miracles that come to my attention. And in part I've come to believe in the power of God to perform miracles because more and more I've seen

God doing remarkable miracles through me and through those I know.

And over the years I have realized that what I am seeing is nothing more nor less than the experience of the early Christians, who had heard their Lord say, "The Kingdom of God is at hand." Jesus Christ performed miracles. The Apostles Peter and Paul performed miracles. Other of the disciples performed miracles. And *you* can perform miracles if you but understand the power of God and the laws of faith and obedience that unlock God's power to those who believe in Him and serve Him.

In essence, that's what the rest of this book is all about: It's an effort to teach some of the basic principles that enable you to understand and experience the flow of God's energy, which moves freely between His Kingdom and our limited, three-dimensional world. So now, let's move ahead and examine what's required for us to establish a powerful personal relationship with God—and to enter the world of miracles—a world that to some seems beyond reason.

CHAPTER TWO

The Miraculous Way to Good Health

God can always heal our bodies when they are damaged or diseased. Sometimes He may just allow the wonderful physical mechanisms He has created—the clotting properties of blood, our natural antibodies, the regenerative qualities of tissue—to take care of any problems by themselves. At other times, though, these natural endowments aren't sufficient: We may be overcome by the disease or injury and find ourselves heading toward permanent disablement or death.

In such situations, God stands ready to intervene in other ways to restore us to good health. In many cases, He wants us to join with Him in the healing process by taking certain "faith steps," which are designed to strengthen our spirits as well as our bodies and minds.

In this chapter and the next, I want to explore some of the specific, miraculous ways that certain individuals have discovered to usher the amazing, healing power of God into their lives. As you'll see, much more may be present in miraculous healings than we are at first aware. Just as God is infinitely complex, so there seems to be a complexity of approaches and combinations of approaches that different people use to achieve healing in their lives.

The miracle of a restored body often begins with a deep, simple personal faith. Sometimes physical healings and other miracles take place instantly, as we'll see at various points in this book. But when you find yourself caught up in the confusing, many-sided details of an actual accident or illness, simplicity often gives way to complexity and variety. So if you hope for a miracle, it's wise to be prepared for an ever-changing, step-by-step journey with God from sickness to health.

But the best way to communicate what physical healings are all about is to show you. So now, let's take a look at several case studies which illustrate in some detail exactly how this special kind of miracle takes place.

The Woman Who Was Persistent in Prayer

When you see Barbara Cummiskey today, it's hard to believe that a relatively short time ago doctors were telling this attractive young woman that she would soon die. They said her condition had become critical and the sixteen-year bout she had been waging with multiple sclerosis was nearing the end.

As it turned out, the doctors were correct—for her long, pain-filled illness *did* come to an abrupt end. But the final phase of the disease wasn't quite what the experts had expected: It terminated not in death, but in victory, in a physical wholeness for Barbara. The way this came about can teach us much about how miraculous healings may occur.

THE MIRACULOUS WAY TO GOOD HEALTH

Before she became ill, Barbara was a vivacious, active teen-ager who was involved in everything from sports to church activities. But when she was fifteen, she started dropping things. She also noticed a tingling sensation in her hands. Her problem was diagnosed as multiple sclerosis, and at this news, her world came crashing down around her.

Her mother recalls the shock of learning about the illness: "I'd heard of MS, but never dreamed it would ever touch anyone in my family. I knew there was someone in the neighborhood who had it, but I didn't realize how bad it was really going to be."

In the years that followed, the Cummiskeys, who live in Wheaton, Illinois, discovered the full extent of the problem their daughter was facing. The disease caused Barbara's hands to curl up, and her legs became so crippled that she was unable to walk. Her vision was blurred to the point of blindness—and all these handicaps marked just the beginning of her troubles.

In describing what her physical condition was like at age fifteen and a half, Barbara says, "Multiple sclerosis is a disease of the central nervous system that affects the brain and spinal cord so that the myelin [the protective sheaths around the cells] is destroyed. It's like destroying the covering of a wire so that the wires hit each other and short out. They start sending wrong messages—or no messages at all—from the brain to the muscles throughout the entire body. The results are paralysis, tremors in the limbs, and vision problems. Also, in severe cases such as mine, the internal organs are [gradually] destroyed."

Over the years, the disease almost completely incapacitated Barbara—to the point where she was paralyzed from the waist down and was confined to bed. She had to have a tracheotomy (a hole cut through her neck to the windpipe) to enable her to breathe. Furthermore, her bladder sphincter stopped functioning, and the doctor had to insert a catheter, or tube, to enable her to urinate. Then her bowels stopped working, and she had to have an ileostomy to take care of that difficulty.

But this still wasn't all. "I was in constant pain, and that meant I needed strong drugs," Barbara said. "Eventually, a pain unit was attached to my chest to fight the pain." She also needed regular suctioning constantly through another machine.

To relieve the isolation of her room, the medical staff occasionally lifted her into an electric wheelchair and rolled her around for short distances. But even on those little trips, she had to remain attached to her oxygen supply and other tubes and devices.

"Finally," Barbara says, "my doctors told me I was going to die."

Under such physical hardship and with her medical outlook so bleak, it would have been easy to become depressed and even to give up hope. But somehow, even at this low point in her illness, Barbara Cummiskey managed to keep her spirits up— and even started back on the road to recovery.

How could such an incredible turnaround take place?

Barbara managed to find a reservoir of supernatural power which grew stronger by the day and eventually brought into her life the miracle of a healed body. The inner healing and growth, which led to outward physical changes, took a number of years and involved a variety of factors and forces. But each step forward in her spiritual life became part of the pattern that God provided for the ultimate recovery.

First of all, even before her illness, Barbara had entered the spiritual world by making a childhood commitment to Christ. She says, "Yes, I knew the Lord. At age nine, I accepted Jesus into my heart as my personal Savior. I grew up in a church where Jesus was really shared. I was active in my church, being president of the youth group."

But then this early commitment lapsed. The first years of Barbara's illness were very hard, physically, emotionally, and spiritually. Although she tried to cope with being constantly sick and with having little control over her life, she became angry and rebellious. Finally, she turned away from Jesus.

But then, when she was about twenty-one, she decided to end her spiritual rebellion and seek solace in God in a more mature way. "A Christian doctor and his wife helped me to see I needed to make a decision for God as an adult," she says. "I needed to dedicate my life as an adult to Jesus—not just Jesus as Savior, but as Lord and Master as well. From that time on, though my physical condition continued to worsen, my spiritual life took on new dimensions."

Spiritual growth became Barbara's main goal, and her prayer life was the centerpiece of that growth. "In the last few years of my illness, with such limited physical capabilities, I cried out to the Lord and asked Him to give me something active to do," she recalled. "He answered and showed me that prayer was [my assignment] and that it can be quite active if we just allow it to be."

As her prayer life deepened, Barbara increasingly reached out to others and the lives of those she encountered were touched profoundly. "I saw some of my roommates in the hospital come to know the Lord," she said. "Sharing Him was really important to me. He had the controls of my life. . . . It was a continuous growing and trusting process."

Despite the fact that her spiritual growth was accelerating with prayer and Bible study, her physical condition was worsening. But even as she grew weaker, Barbara became more sensitive to God's presence in her life. She learned to "hear" and "know" the Lord's voice when He spoke to her innermost being—as if He were talking clearly and directly to her.

One person who watched her spiritual growth was her pastor, who visited her frequently in the hospital. "During that period," he noted, "in the midst of the suffering, I could see the development of her spiritual life. She lay in bed and talked to the Lord. Sometimes you'd walk into the room and hear her talking to Him."

A faith that can bring miracles into a person's life involves this sort of individual confrontation with Christ and personal commitment to Him. But in Barbara's case, there was more: The broader Christian community participated in bearing her burden. So Barbara wasn't the only one who was communicating to God in prayer. People throughout her locality were praying for her as a result of a report on her condition carried by a local religious radio program. Listeners were invited to pray for her and write to her if they wished, and soon she received hundreds of letters and cards.

With this kind of spiritual support and commitment, the stage was set for a miracle. Jesus had been Barbara's steady companion for years, and her heart and spirit had come to recognize His voice even when there was no audible sound. In this spiritual dimension she had entered, she had a heightened sensitivity to His will for her life. She was ready to hear the direction He wanted her to take, and she was also ready to obey.

On Sunday, June 7, 1981, Barbara was lying in bed at home with her ever-present oxygen tank in place. Her aunt and two other women from the Wheaton Wesleyan Church were reading to her some mail from radio listeners. Then, in that setting, all those seeds of prayer and spiritual growth that had been planted finally came to fruition. She tells the story best in her own words:

"I heard God tell me, 'My child, get up and walk!' I immediately shared [with those present] what I had heard, and I told them to hurry and get my family. Since God had told me to get up and walk—in spite of everything—I knew I would. I *jumped* out of bed, minus the oxygen, and walked! In literally a twinkling of an eye, He totally healed me from a severe illness of sixteen years' duration!"

Barbara's muscles had shriveled during those sixteen years when she had been confined to her bed and wheelchair most of the time. But after she got out of bed and started walking, she looked down at her hands and legs. They were filled out and completely restored. She ran to meet her mother and father who had responded to her call, and what a celebration there was!

That night, just to confirm her healing, she put on high-heeled sandals and went to church. At the service, she praised the Lord with her friends who had been praying for her for years. "What a sharing we had!" she says.

The next day, Barbara called her doctor, Dr. Thomas Marshall, and made an appointment to see him at his office. The appointment in itself was quite a feat because she had been homebound for previous checkups, and the doctor had been required to visit her. In fact, she hadn't even been out of the house for two years except to go to the hospital by ambulance.

When the doctor checked her, she said, "No signs of disease were present. My lungs were now whole and working properly with the diaphragm pumping normally. The tube in my throat was pulled out; the catheter was removed; the pain unit was taken off; and all medication was discontinued. But most important of all, the doctor gave God the credit!"

Afterward, Dr. Marshall appeared on a television program where Barbara told of her healing. In describing her visit to his office that day, he said, "At first, I thought it was a lookalike and wasn't really Barb. But after speaking for a few minutes, it obviously *was* her, and she had had a miraculous healing of her MS symptoms. She was sitting and walking normally. Although the tracheotomy [tube] was in [her throat], it was obvious that her breathing was improved because she spoke much more clearly, with more force. So we proceeded to take out the [tube]."

Barbara is now leading a full, active life and is studying to be a surgical technician. She is frequently invited to discuss her tremendous healing at churches and meetings of those afflicted by multiple sclerosis. She often tells them that God is definitely alive—and He is still working great miracles on this earth. After all, she is living proof. But she always adds, "To God be the glory because this is His doing, and in fact, His story—not mine. I've done nothing to earn or deserve what He has done for me, and especially this miracle."

But even as we stand amazed at this miracle, some may ask a very logical question: Why did it take sixteen years for God to answer all those prayers that were said for Barbara?

I certainly don't have all the answers. But I do know that Jesus placed great emphasis on the power of *persistence* in prayer. For example, in Luke 11:5–10, He told the story of a man who went to a friend's house at midnight to borrow three loaves of bread. Even though the occupants were long in bed, the needy supplicant persisted until his needs were met. In the Living Bible, Jesus is quoted as saying, "[If] you keep knocking long enough he will get up and give you everything you want—just because of your persistence. And so it is with prayer—keep on asking and you will keep on getting. . . ."

Similarly, in Luke 18:1–8, Jesus tells the story of an unjust judge, who finally gives a woman what she wants because she keeps after him. "People ought always to pray and not lose heart," Christ says.

Barbara Cummiskey and her family and friends heeded this principle by praying constantly for most of sixteen years, and God responded with a great miracle of healing. Obviously, much more was involved in her recovery than just persistence in prayer. But if you had to pick one key lesson from her experience, the power of long-term prayer would probably be that lesson. Still, everyone's case is just a little different, and so, as might be expected, there are other principles to be learned from our next story.

The Beauty Queen Who Built an Inner Fortress of Faith

During her late teens, Kathy Kovacs seemed to have everything going for her. She had received a number of assignments as a model. Entering beauty contests, she had managed to win eleven pageant titles, including "Miss Henry Ford College 1966–67" and "Miss United Nations 1966–67." And romance was not far behind. Kathy began dating Dave Kovacs, a medical student who, as a graduate physician, became her husband.

But in those days, God wasn't a part of Kathy and Dave's life. They lived and loved much as other young people from their age and background. She was pregnant before they were married, and they opted for an abortion. Their life-style—at least at the time—didn't seem to interfere with their happiness. After their wedding, they settled down in Three Rivers, Michigan, where Dave began to practice emergency and trauma medicine. A seemingly unclouded future lay before this beautiful young woman and her talented husband. But then things started to go wrong.

During their first years of marriage, Kathy began to have arthritic pain in her joints. Before long, the pain increased and there was tremendous swelling. Despite these physical problems, Kathy very much wanted to have children, and soon she became pregnant. But then she miscarried and had difficulty conceiving again.

With his medical background, Dave suspected something might be seriously wrong with Kathy, and so he began running laboratory tests on his own. He discovered evidences of systemic lupus erythematosus, an inflammatory disease of the connective tissue that supports and protects all parts of the body. When lupus strikes, the immune system goes out of kilter and produces antibodies that attack healthy tissue.

Devastated, Dave decided to check with a specialist who told him the laboratory findings might be a false alarm. So Dave elected not to tell Kathy about his suspicions. He answered her questions about her illness by saying, "You have a nonspecific type of arthritis."

The couple continued to want children, and they kept trying. "After much effort, lab work, and infertility work-ups, I finally conceived," Kathy said. "I delivered a healthy boy in September 1974, and our second son was born in July 1976."

During the first pregnancy there were minimal complications, and the doctors were still not sure if she had lupus. But during the second pregnancy, there were more problems. In fact, Kathy was afraid she might not be able to carry the child to term. She did manage to make it through the birth, but about six weeks later, Kathy became incurably ill with lupus.

The symptoms were deadly: There was progressive damage to her kidneys, crippling arthritic pain, skin lesions on her face and other parts of the body, and tremendous fatigue. When Dave and their doctor informed her, she was crushed—and angry at Dave for not letting her know his suspicions about the disease when they had first occurred to him.

"I don't know if you can imagine how I felt," she now says. "I had known relatively good health and been able to give birth to my second baby. But then [I experienced] the degeneration of my body to the point where it was riddled with pain, swollen joints, and enormous fatigue. Also, my face was a scabby mess. I remember the horror of being told I was incurably ill—and even if I made it into remission, I would be sick and afflicted for the rest of my life."

By this time Kathy was thoroughly depressed and discouraged. She had been married for only six years, and yet she was sick and tired all the time. She couldn't do what she wanted to do for her two young boys. But still she didn't give up. To find out more about the disease, she started plowing through Dave's medical books. After reading them, she said, "I realized there was no cure for lupus—only drugs and more drugs, fear and more fear, and not knowing what the next day would bring."

In an effort to find some solution, Dave and Kathy went from one doctor to the next, but none of them had any adequate treatment to offer. So Dave took it upon himself to treat her. He placed her on high dosages of steroids, narcotics, and other drugs—many of which had unpleasant side effects.

Before her sickness, Kathy had been so obsessed with her beauty-queen looks that she refused to appear in public—even to guests in her home—without makeup and hair styling that took up to two hours. Now her treasured looks had vanished: She became almost bald and grew a downy beard and mustache. Her chest, back, arms, and legs grew very hairy. Her breasts lost all muscle tone and hung down on her chest. Among the most obvious disfigurements were the plantar warts that covered her face: They became so numerous that they actually overlapped in some areas. She also started losing her eyebrows and eyelashes. Her eyelids were covered by blisterlike bubbles, her vision became blurry, her hearing deteriorated, and her teeth loosened.

The drug dosage was so high during this period that she suffered from excruciating headaches. Perhaps most disturbing, it became impossible for her to think and reason clearly. At times she forgot her own name and address; her speech became slurred; she was frequently housebound because bright sunlight could trigger further complications.

Kathy continued to search for answers, but hope was slowly ebbing away. She remembers asking Dave, "How much longer can I go on?"

But he wouldn't answer her, and she knew what that meant. She said, "Because of Dave's strong sense of integrity and honesty, he wouldn't falsely lead me to believe that I was going to live, when I wasn't."

Despair overtook her, and she wondered if it was worthwhile to go on: "The suffering and mental torment were too intense," she recalls. "There was the torment of seeing myself totally disfigured and of being too tired and weak to care for my baby. Also, knowing that you'll probably be replaced as a wife and mother hurts terribly. Not that you wouldn't want your husband to remarry—but rather you want to be the one to share his life and mother his children."

As she neared the lowest spiritual and emotional ebb in her life, Kathy even tried to take her life. She said she just wanted out—no more pain, suffering, and crying. She also thought she was having a harmful effect on the lives of her husband and her children.

But then a change started to occur—a truly miraculous change sparked by an influx of faith that finally helped her begin to pull her life together again. Here are the faith steps that Kathy experienced as she steadily and systematically developed a healing relationship with God:

Step 1: Other people were praying for her. Even when she was at her sickest, Kathy remembers, people told her they were praying for her recovery. "If people [like me] start praying, you know it's serious. I didn't know the Lord, and when people said they were praying for me, I thought, 'That's nice, but what's that going to get me?' Up until that time my conception of God was as a distant deity: If you were good, you went to heaven; and if you were bad, you went to hell."

Step 2: Kathy began to search for God. The lowest point in her life came, as she remembers it, when "I was confronted with multiple diseases that no man on this earth could take away, and I was broken in every possible way, physically and mentally." It was at this breaking point that God's love somehow began to get through to her. Even as her condition deteriorated, she began "an active search for the living Christ—whom I did not even know was real."

She watched religious television programs, listened to Christian music, and read the Bible. And she started to realize that beyond any question, she "needed a miracle that could come only through the hands of God."

"I was beginning to understand that Jesus truly lives on this earth, and He wants me healthy. I saw that I was sick because I was outside of God's protection and was experiencing the work of Satan in my body and mind."

Step 3: She "prayed for the best" for herself. Even though she was still searching for God, she had enough faith to "pray for the best" for herself: That is, she asked Him for abundant health, and nothing in between!

Step 4: Kathy committed her life to Christ. Finally, Kathy realized that the answer to all her problems lay in God's plan for salvation. So by faith she accepted Jesus Christ, God's Son, as her personal Lord and Savior.

Step 5: Kathy confessed her past and present sins—and asked for forgiveness. Both Kathy and Dave knew down deep that having that abortion before they got married was wrong. But at the time it happened, they had a big wedding coming up, and they simply didn't want to spoil their plans by having her pregnant at the time. So they took what they thought was the "easy" route out of that predicament. After her commitment to Christ, Kathy recognized she had been wrong in this case, and she confessed that transgression to God.

Also, she asked to be forgiven for her bitterness and resentment toward her husband for not telling her the truth about her sickness when he first suspected it. She had tried to forgive and forget, but it took the power of the Holy Spirit, after her commitment to Christ, for the hurts and memories to be healed.

Step 6: Another Christian prayed for her healing, and she acted in faith on this prayer. A minister she knew called her on the phone, and in that conversation, she recalls, "He commanded Satan to leave me and prayed that I would be restored as though the disease had never entered my body." He also gave her some Scriptures to memorize and told her to go downstairs and tell her husband that she was healed. Obediently, she went down and told Dave she had been healed—even though she felt he probably would think she was crazy.

Step 7: God provided a physical signal that He was at work. A few seconds after she informed her husband she had been healed, Kathy said she experienced "a warm, intense heat deep within my shoulder. It lasted about five minutes and then disappeared. It was beautiful, and from that moment on, [most of my] fear of dying and never being normal again was gone. God had touched my body, and I knew it!"

(I've noticed in other cases that a feeling of heat frequently accompanies miraculous healings. This sensation is apparently a physical signal that God sometimes provides to let us know He has heard our pleas and is working in our bodies.)

Step 8: Kathy expanded her community of prayer partners. Among other things, she called one of our CBN counseling centers and the counselor not only prayed for a complete healing, but gave her the biblical encouragement needed for her faith to grow.

Step 9: She studied the Scriptures for passages and promises about healing. The working of miracles, including healings, is certainly rooted in faith and trust in God. But at the same time, God honors our efforts to understand more about Him and how He can work supernaturally in our lives—and this is where Bible study comes in. It just stands to reason that the more you know about a subject, the better you're going to be at applying it in practical situations. The same principle applies to miraculous healings.

So Kathy started searching the Scriptures for passages on healing. Because of her disease, she says, "the only information and knowledge I could retain was that of the Scriptures. I couldn't remember my name and address, but God allowed His living Word to be established in my heart and mind."

Step 10: Kathy filled her time with spiritually uplifting thoughts and activities. The Apostle Paul says in Philippians 4:8: ". . . whatever is true, whatever is noble, whatever is right, whatever is pure, whatever is lovely, whatever is admirable—if anything is excellent or praiseworthy—think about such things."

Similarly, Kathy says, "I prayed constantly and played tapes concerning healing and why some people are not healed." As a new Christian, she was aware that she had a great deal to learn.

She particularly wanted to understand how to walk in faith—how to believe God's Word and promises, even if she couldn't see any immediate physical results. By focusing on uplifting verses, tapes, and books, she found it was much easier to accomplish this goal.

Step 11: A loved one established a relationship with the Lord. The more we surround ourselves with praying believers, the more spiritual power we seem able to generate to accomplish miracles. In Kathy's case, extra prayer power came into her life when her mother turned her life over to Christ. Shortly after this commitment, her mother even went to church and, as an intermediary for Kathy, had other believers lay their hands on her seven times. She wanted hands laid on her six times, one for each physical malady she had observed in Kathy. Also, she asked for the laying on of hands the seventh time as a request that God would give her daughter a special gift of faith, so that Kathy would believe she really could be healed.

Furthermore, Kathy says, God responded with a definite answer: "He gave me that gift of faith—a faith that could move my mountain of disease." Filled with the Holy Spirit, she felt new hope spring up inside her as a result of her mother's actions.

Step 12: Kathy began to "claim" the promises of Scripture. It's fascinating to me how many passages of the Bible contain direct promises that God makes to us. Try reading through a book such as Proverbs, and see how many times God tells us that He will do certain things for us if we just ask Him to. Unfortunately, though, many of us never reach the level of faith where we feel confident in "claiming" those promises that God has made to us.

But Kathy Kovacs *did* develop that degree of faith—perhaps as a result of the "gift" of faith she had received after her mother's actions on her behalf. As she read the Bible regularly, she began to focus on certain promises, and she didn't hesitate to ask God to fulfill them. Here are a few:

- "By His stripes I am healed." (Isaiah 53:5)
- "Beloved, I wish above all things that you may prosper and be in health even as thy soul prospers." (III John 2)
- "Whatever you ask in my name, I will do it, that the Father may be glorified in the Son." (John 14:13)
- "Whosoever shall say unto this mountain [this disease?] be thou removed and cast into the sea and shall not doubt in his heart, it shall be done unto him." (Matthew 21:21)

It's important to remember that even after taking all these steps, Kathy was still deep in the grip of the disease. But despite how she felt and looked as a result of the lupus, she continued to rely on God's promises. And she believed by faith that she had *already* been healed. "This was not a matter of the power of positive thinking, or mind over matter," she notes. "Rather, it was positively affirming what God's Word says about me and allowing God's power and healing to flow."

Step 13: As medical tests showed that healing had begun, Kathy immediately increased her reliance on God. Finally, the long-expected day arrived when Kathy's laboratory tests began to reflect normal results. As a consequence, the doctor reduced her drug dosages. But soon after this good news, Kathy demonstrated her willingness to risk even more on Christ: She felt Him tell her to go off the drugs completely. Still, though, Kathy was cautious. Before she took this action, she asked Dave for a medical opinion of what might happen if she ignored the drugs.

"If you're healed, there's nothing to be afraid of," he said matter-of-factly. "If you are not, taking the drugs away will cause the disease to rise above the drug level and become active again. Your body will not be able to stand another assault—and you'll die."

That was certainly a clear-cut analysis of her situation. But she decided to go with her inner assurances and get rid of the drugs. Then, if she continued to improve, "I would know that I was healed and not [merely] in remission."

The important thing here is that Kathy *knew*, beyond any doubt, that God had told her she was healed and the drugs were no longer necessary. If she had refused the drugs and taken the risk just for the sake of the risk, that would have been foolhardy. But if we are truly walking with God, a potentially frightening situation is not really risky at all because Jesus is at our side and will not ask us to do anything that will harm our minds or bodies.

So Kathy followed that inner leading, and God upheld her. "After I went off the drugs, I no longer needed any naps, and I had more strength and energy than I had ever known," she said.

Step 14: She continued to trust God and praise Him as final healing occurred. Even after you're over the worst in a bad illness, it's important not to let down spiritually. In fact, we become most vulnerable after we've seen some successes because we begin to expect things to go along easily and smoothly.

But Kathy didn't make this mistake. Some symptoms and side effects of the disease lingered even after the drugs were removed, but she remained confident that they would all eventually be cleared up. "I could rejoice knowing that my God would not put me to shame and leave me partially healed," she said confidently.

Two or three months later, as she continued to praise and thank God for the complete healing she knew was coming, the warts and skin lesions she still suffered from disappeared—literally overnight! She says she felt "supreme joy" when she could stand before her mirror and wash her face without seeing or feeling those ugly blemishes. For the first time in about two years, Kathy once again had healthy, smooth skin.

Now the other effects of lupus have also disappeared. Kathy's hair is darker, thicker, and curlier than ever before, and her vision and hearing are back to normal. "Also, I have no pain, no arthritis, and no fatigue," she says. "Glory to God!"

After she had taken her final laboratory test, Kathy shared her faith in Jesus as her healer with her doctor, technician, and nurses. She told them explicitly that Christ had healed her. Then, when she walked out into the parking lot, she was filled with an ineffable sense of joy. "I stood quietly by myself, with tears filling my eyes, and I knew that God had chosen me to live, to be healthy for His glory."

Almost involuntarily, her heart and mind uttered the words, "It is over; it is finished. The battle has been won, for Christ won the victory for me."

Kathy's victory seems to have come as a result of a gradual building up of an immovable foundation of faith. If she had experienced a quick healing, the beneficial changes and growth in her spirit might never have occurred. And so God apparently chose this step-by-step method to build her spiritual life at the same time that he was healing her body.

It is basic to understand that God's primary concern centers in our spiritual lives and our personal relationship with Him. Jesus said it best: "What does it profit a man to gain the whole world and lose his own soul?"

God will remove temporal blessings if these things serve to blight our spiritual lives. And He will add temporal blessings in abundance when they draw us to Him.

Special Communication

God knows all things. There are wonderful times when He shares a bit of His knowledge—a "word of knowledge" as the Apostle Paul called it—with His people. This is intelligence that comes from God without reliance on sight, sound, taste, touch, or smell. Often God will use such a revelation to describe a condition affecting an individual. Then He gives the good news that a miraculous answer is taking place in the individual's life.

Over the years I have personally experienced thousands of such words of knowledge and have witnessed the joy that comes from the recipients. One of the most striking examples involved a North Carolina pastor, Clay Davis, and his son, Mike, who works for the Christian Broadcasting Network.

Clay had suffered two heart attacks, and medical checkups in 1977 revealed that the left side of his heart had become enlarged, with malfunctioning valves. After the attacks, he gradually began to recuperate and went back to his full-time duties as a minister. But the chest pains returned in the fall of 1980, and this time they were so severe that he had to give up most of his routine activities.

Clay desperately wanted to continue preaching, however, and so he tried to conserve his strength by resting much of each day and then taking over his pulpit twice a week. Unfortunately, things didn't work out quite as he had planned. "I got quite sick in the middle of preaching one day, and I didn't think I would get through it," he recalls.

His elders prayed for him after this incident, and he also went in for some extra medical tests. After the checkup, his doctor scheduled him for a catheterization on January 27, 1981, to determine the exact location of certain clogged arteries—and also to prepare him for open-heart surgery. Because Clay had been praying for a healing, he was naturally disappointed to learn that this procedure would be necessary.

Yet, he says, "I had the greatest peace ever known. We prayed before the Lord, and the peace of God came in." Specifically, he and his Christian friends asked God to heal his heart condition *during* the heart catheterization.

So, what happened on that fateful January 27?

"They didn't find anything!" Clay says. "Early the next morning, the doctor walked into my room and threw the charts down on the bed. He said, 'I can't find anything wrong.' I knew God's hand was in what had happened."

His chest pains soon disappeared, and his energy returned. According to his wife, "Overnight, when Clay came home from the hospital, he was a different person."

But there's more: As a confirmation of what He had done, God provided Clay with an incontrovertible word of knowledge, which occurred this way:

My *700 Club* co-host, Ben Kinchlow, and I had been praying on the air, and each of us was given a word of knowledge by the Holy Spirit. My special message went like this: "Someone . . . has a heart that is enlarged, and God is causing that heart to resume its normal size in your chest cavity—and it's just miraculous what is happening."

That program was taped, and the Reverend Clay Davis's son saw it when it aired a few weeks later. Immediately, he says, "I just knew that it was my dad. So I checked the date on which the program was recorded. It was January 27, 1981—the day my father was in the hospital!"

But Mike didn't stop there in his research: "Then I checked the computer for the *time* the word of knowledge was recorded and found it was eleven-twenty-four A.M. My dad was on the operating table between eleven and twelve that day!"

Just to be sure, Mike drove up to see his father, and his family verified that the time I had spoken the word of knowledge was the *exact* period when Clay had been in the operating room. "Then we knew it was real," Mike says. Clay had prayed that he would be healing *during* his heart catheterization, and apparently his heart resumed its normal size at about that time.

Today, Pastor Clay Davis is full of energy and is no longer slowed up by a heart problem. His visible good health and his willingness to testify freely about his healing have helped strengthen the faith of other members of his congregation. And he remains a dramatic example of how God may sometimes place his undeniable seal on a miraculous healing by issuing a special message to one of those who has entered His Secret Kingdom.

With God, the Impossible Is Always Possible

Sometimes, when tragedy strikes those who are closest to us, it's easy to give up hope. An accident, disease, or other misfortune may be so devastating that it seems to us that nothing or no one—not even God—can turn things around. But a major message of the Gospel is that with God, *nothing* is impossible—absolutely nothing. (See Matthew 19:26.) That's an important principle to keep in mind when the outlook for the future seems bleakest.

An illustration of this point comes through in a problem that confronted the Paul Burak family, who live near Fort Lauderdale, Florida. One night in early May 1979, Barbara Burak heard her nine-year-old son, Paul junior, call to her in panic: "I can't see—and my head hurts!" He had been suffering from an ear infection, and now his condition had become much worse. Sobbing, the youngster told his mother he couldn't even focus his eyes.

This event marked the beginning of their nightmare. Within twenty-four hours, Barbara and Paul had rushed Paul junior to a hospital in Miami—because of a diagnosis of encephalitis. The boy was in critical condition and was not expected to live.

The people at the Buraks' church started a prayer chain and began to pray continuously around the clock. "We had people praying all over the country," Barbara recalls. Of course, it would have been easy just to give up and sink into despair. But as far as God is concerned, the Buraks don't know the meaning of the word *impossible.*

Paul junior remained in a coma for four days and then stayed semicomatose for fifteen more days. His condition went up and down. Sometimes it seemed hopeful; other times, hopeless. Barbara couldn't bear to see her son suffer like this, and so she went off alone to talk to God in prayer. She told the Lord she wasn't losing her faith, but she emphasized that He had to help her and give her the strength to get through this ordeal. "You have to help that boy!" she prayed. "You can't let him come out of this a vegetable!"

A definite answer to this prayer seemed to come the next morning, when an EEG showed normal results. But the tough times weren't over by any means. A CAT scan the following day showed what a doctor described as "definite brain damage." But when Paul senior heard this report, his faith in God's ability to overcome the impossible seemed to grow even stronger. He said, "The Lord has kept him alive this long. He's brought him this far. He's going to perform a miracle, and He doesn't do halfway jobs." As for the diagnosis of brain damage, he said flatly, "*I'm not going to accept it!*"

These weren't hollow words, either. From that point, when his father took such an unwavering stand on faith, Paul junior began to recover. His improvement baffled the doctors, but the boy knew the source of his help: He told anyone who would listen that it was Jesus who was healing him. Finally, he recovered totally, in defiance of a doctor's prediction that he would be mentally impaired. A child neurologist has confirmed that he's completely well, and since his release from the hospital, he's been an A student in school.

In short, the lesson from the Buraks' experience is that it's never wise to accept any physical condition as "impossible" to heal. In fact, the first step in tackling an "impossible" problem is to recognize that with God all things—absolutely all—are possible.

Responding to the Needs of Others Brought Healing

With glaucoma, there may be few if any warning signs. Gradually, a person's side vision disappears, and then central vision goes. That's how blindness sneaked up on Clyde Bass of Tulsa, Oklahoma.

After his doctors discovered the disease, Clyde's vision deteriorated until he could see only shadows and vague outlines of objects—no details of features. Finally, he became totally blind. In an effort to adjust to his new world of darkness, Clyde acquired a Braille watch, a white cane, and a Library of Congress record player. He could go outside only if someone who could see took him.

A veteran of World War II, Clyde had developed a limp after suffering a war injury, and that disability, coupled with his blindness, threatened his mobility still further. "I was pretty lonesome and had a kind of 'downward' look on life," he says. "It was so dark. I felt very low and knew that I needed help—and that it had to come from above."

A series of personal faith steps brought a rather dramatic form of help into Clyde's life.

Step One: Early Christian influences had the first impact. As a youngster, Clyde had accepted Jesus as his Savior, but over the years he had drifted away from the Lord. Still, the early religious training proved valuable. Since Clyde could no longer see to read, he needed recorded material and went to the First United Methodist Church in Tulsa to see if they had cassette tapes that he could use on his recorder. This initial contact led him to join the church, and he began attending services regularly.

Step Two: Clyde was persistent in his prayers. For three years after the onset of glaucoma, Clyde struggled in the unfamiliar world of dark shadows. But he really believed in miracles, and every day he asked God to restore his sight.

It may seem strange—especially to those who don't have any physical problems—that God would especially honor regular requests of this type. Why shouldn't He just respond to the first supplication? Why bestow any greater blessing on those who ask over and over again for the same thing?

As I indicated in the case of Barbara Cummiskey's healing, I don't pretend to have all the answers to these questions. But I do know that persistent prayer is part of God's plan for helping us develop a solid relationship with Him. Perhaps He knows that if we continue to talk to Him about a particular problem or concern, we'll come to understand our own needs, and our own relationship with Him better. It's not so much that persistent prayer will change God's mind. Rather, persistent prayer changes us and draws us into a closer relationship with God.

In any case, Clyde continued to persevere in prayer, and this commitment was a cornerstone for the great things that eventually happened to him.

Step Three: He encouraged others to pray for him. Clyde was quite lonely, and he found the *700 Club* counseling center in Tulsa to be a godsend. It gave him access to people with spiritual understanding—a group of patient, Spirit-filled friends whom he could call upon and pray with.

He often phoned the local center, and one of our counselors related, "When Clyde would call *The 700 Club* for prayer, we would agree with him according to what the Scriptures say. We would just trust together with him that God would do what He said He could do in restoring sight."

In this connection, you'll remember that when Jesus announced His ministry in the synagogue at Nazareth, he read from Isaiah, saying, "The Spirit of the Lord is upon me, because he has anointed me to preach good news to the poor. He has sent me to proclaim release to the captives and recovering of sight to the blind, to set at liberty those who are oppressed, to proclaim the acceptable year of the Lord." And then, Jesus concluded, "Today this scripture has been fulfilled in your hearing." (Luke 4:18–21)

Step Four: Clyde gave generously to God's work. Although he had a limited income, Clyde knew that the Bible encourages giving—and so he became a "cheerful giver." In fact, this decision to give seemed to be the spiritual trigger that led directly to his healing. After hearing of the needs of a particular Christian organization, he called and made a substantial pledge of his income. Immediately after he hung up the phone, fluid began to drain from his eyes, and an excruciating pain burned through them. He went directly to the Lord with his problem, and in his own words, here's what happened next:

"I said, 'Lord, I just can't stand this!' It was hurting so bad that I got on my knees and began to pray. I cried to the Lord and said, 'My God is able! My God is able to restore vision!' And I wanted that. Then I felt His presence in my room."

When he finally finished praying, he felt as though he had entered a different world. And not only that—he could see!

Nine months after his dramatic healing, Clyde returned to his ophthalmologist for a checkup, and he made a stunning discovery: Clyde was told that he still had glaucoma, even though his vision was 20/20. Previously, his sight had been 20/200. He still wears glasses, but they are only to correct his farsightedness.

His doctor, Richard E. Mills, D.O., said this about his condition: "It is difficult for me, as a physician, to determine whether or not the change in visual acuity was subjective or objective. I have no test which will allow me to make this determination. There is, however, the possibility that Mr. Bass may have had a nonophthalmic healing which certainly would be applicable in his case."

In other words, he had been healed through means other than the normal physical healing of his eyes. But the inability of medical science to explain exactly what has happened doesn't bother Clyde at all. He now has his driver's license, and he frequently volunteers his time to transport those who need a lift somewhere. Moreover, he's given away his Braille watch, his wraparound glasses, and his white guide stick.

Clearly, there were a number of spiritual factors that accompanied Clyde Bass's miraculous recovery from glaucoma. But perhaps the most striking—and the one most closely connected in time to his healing—was that decision to give of himself and his substance. This phenomenon, which I've called the Law of Reciprocity in my book *The Secret Kingdom*, has its biblical roots in Luke 6:38, where Jesus enunciated it most clearly,

"Give and it will be given unto you, pressed down, good measure, running over. . . ."

The Secret of "Soaking Prayer"

The practice of "soaking prayer" involves bringing out the heavy spiritual artillery of overwhelming prayer support for an individual. It's not just a matter of saying, "Let us pray for so-and-so," and then perhaps uttering a short prayer and forgetting about the needy individual or situation for several days, a week or more. Rather, soaking prayer is a way of immersing the individual or concern in a veritable *ocean* of prayer support.

An excellent example of this principle was the experience of nine-year-old Kevin Juhl, who started suffering from severe headaches. His family doctor ordered a CAT scan and an EEG, and the result revealed a brain tumor over an extensive area. Kevin was referred to a neurologist, who confirmed the diagnosis and informed the family that the tumor was a slow-growing but very persistent variety of killer.

The youngster was put on steroids in an effort to reduce the swelling in his brain, and another CAT scan was scheduled two months later. In the meantime, however, Kevin's parents decided to launch a soaking-prayer assault on the growth. In fact, Kevin's mother, Karen, was so sure of the power of the prayer they planned that she told the neurologist, "When the scan is done two months from now, it will be clean because I *know* Jesus will heal Kevin!"

Here, then, is the approach Kevin's parents relied upon:

First of all, Kevin was surrounded by prayers. His family, members of their church, and people throughout the community joined in this massive prayer effort. Karen said, "I was scared, but I just truly believed God's will would be done, and Kevin would be healed."

Next, some Christians laid their hands on Kevin, prayed for his recovery, and rebuked Satan. The elders of their church were the first to begin to lay hands on Kevin on a regular basis. Also, Ben Kinchlow, my associate on *The 700 Club*, spoke at a church near the Juhls' home, and Karen took Kevin to hear him. After Ben had finished his talk, Karen asked him to pray for Kevin: "Ben laid hands on Kevin and called Satan a liar; and he bound up the tumor in the name of Jesus and cast it out."

Ben then gave Karen some follow-up instructions: He told her to lay her hands on Kevin every night and "speak" to the tumor by ordering it out of the boy, calling Satan a liar, and focusing on the atoning, healing work of Jesus on the cross. "I did that every night without fail," Karen said.

But this immersion in prayer was just part of a much broader spiritual program. Typically, when a healing occurs, there is evidence of deep faith in the one who needs healing, as well as in those who are praying for him. And young Kevin certainly had the kind of faith that God requires. "Praying is the best thing anyone can do for me," the boy said at one point. The lack of fear in Karen and her husband, Ken, and their trust in Jesus, was reflected in Kevin's thinking and in his attitude about his illness.

So, what was the result of this soaking-prayer effort?

When Kevin went in for his second CAT scan, it was completely clean. There was no indication of anything abnormal, and no sign of the brain tumor that had been there two months before. Karen's response to the good news was to place credit where credit was due: "Praise the Lord!" she said.

Their family doctor told a television audience, "I can't . . . There is just nothing to explain it. The child never received any medicine or radiation—just prayer." The first CAT scan, he said, was "extremely abnormal with a very large tumor in the parietal lobe on the left." In contrast, the second CAT scan "showed that the tumor had totally disappeared. I have copies of both the before and after CAT scans. I have no doubt that this child was healed because of the prayers of his mother and the many others who prayed for him."

The doctor was also asked, "What are the chances that the tumor could have just gone away or been medically healed, and that it wasn't a miraculous healing?"

"I've never seen anything like that go away," the doctor said. "Brain tumors just do not disappear in a short period of time."

In some cases, God may heal a person instantaneously. Or He may choose to heal or perform other supernatural acts over a period of time. His reasons for the approach He picks may not be immediately apparent. But we can always be sure that He picks the recovery that will be in our best interests.

Sometimes we need to have Him work with us over a long period of time so that He can build up important areas of faith where we are weak. At other times, the divine purpose in our lives may not be clear at all. But in every case, if we have committed our problems to Him, we can be sure He is working them out in a way that, in the long run, will benefit us as much as possible.

As we've seen, physical healings may be triggered in a variety of ways. Some of the most common I've encountered, many of which have been described in the foregoing illustrations, are:

- *Praying specifically for God to act in a certain way.*
  Many times, a healing takes place after a person asks
  God in clear-cut terms to perform a miracle. Some-
  times, the specific prayer may come from a third per-

son who offers an "intercessory prayer," which requests another's healing.

- *Laying on of hands.* Sometimes a minister, the elders of a church, or other believers will place their hands on the sick person and pray for him. (See Acts 3:6–8.)
- *Anointing with oil.* On other occasions, the touching will be done by placing oil on the ailing person. (See James 5:14.)
- *"Rebuking" an evil spirit of infirmity.* On a number of occasions, Jesus saw that a physical problem was caused by the active forces of evil directed by Satan. As a result, He commanded Satan or the evil spirit under Satan's control to leave the person, that is, He "rebuked" the evil spirit. (See Matthew 9:32–33; 12:22–28.)
- *A gradual building and strengthening of the individual's faith.* Quite often, a physical problem begins to disappear as the individual deepens his own spiritual life. The complete healing may come when there is a breakthrough in one particular area of spiritual development—like discovering the joy of generous giving, as we saw in one of the examples above. In such cases, God apparently uses the gradual or delayed healing of the disability as a vehicle to draw the person closer to Him.

So these six spiritual case studies illustrate many things about the healing of seemingly incurable illnesses. But they are by no means the only channels God uses to perform miracles in the human body. As you can see from the faith steps I've outlined in several of these cases, the relationships that human beings establish with the Lord prior to these healings are often comprehensive and profound.

Almighty God is infinite, all powerful, all knowing, yet as the Apostle Paul reminds us, "His ways are past finding out." Clearly there can be no mechanical formula or gimmick that a human being can employ in seeking God. Prayer, above all, is the relationship of our human spirit with the Spirit of God. Prayer is loving, trusting, hoping, surrender—not a set of rules. So I would suggest that you regard these examples and the principles they reveal more as pointers to establishing a deep faith than as hard-and-fast models or rules that can be applied mechanistically to damaged or diseased bodies.

Now as a further guide to bringing the miraculous power of God into your body, let's see how recovery can occur after the ravages of perhaps the most devastating killer of all—cancer.

CHAPTER THREE

The Conquest of Cancer

Cancer is one of the greatest killers in the world.

Characterized by an uncontrolled growth and spread of abnormal cells in the body, this disease almost always results in death if it's not checked. Cancer strikes two out of three American families, and about 440,000 Americans are expected to die from its ravages in 1984. Cancer also kills more children in the three- to fourteen-year-age range than any other malady.

Some 885,000 people were diagnosed as having cancer in 1983, according to the American Cancer Society. Many of them will survive because of standard medical treatments such as surgery, X rays, radioactive substances, chemicals, hormones, and immunotherapy.

But in addition, some people are completely healed of cancer in ways that medical science simply can't explain. This is another point at which the marvelous world of miracles enters our own limited, three-dimensional existence. I personally know of hundreds of people whose cancer was diagnosed as terminal but who have been miraculously healed.

Of course, those who have received divine healings amount to only a small fraction of the total number who are stricken with cancer each year. But I firmly believe that many more could be restored to health in this way if only they would learn to enter the miracle dimension which is open to all of us. Now, to see some of the ways a cancer patient can receive healing power by entering God's supernatural realm of reality, let's examine a few real-life situations.

The Power of Total Faith

When Kirt Hadick was a freshman in high school in Santa Maria, California, he went to the doctor to have a growth examined. His mother, Sue Hadick, stuck close to him as he was shuttled quickly from one specialist and one round of examinations to another.

Worry always plagues a family in a situation like this. But at the same time, they still hold on to the hope that there's nothing really wrong. In Kirt's case, though, a great deal was wrong. When the results were in, he was diagnosed as having "embryonal carcinoma of the testis"—or cancer of the testicles, for which there is no known cure.

There was hardly time for the blow to sink in before the surgery schedule was set up. But after several operations, the cancer continued to spread through Kirt's lymphatic system. The doctors finally told Kirt the bad news: He had terminal cancer.

The hospital's tumor board told the Hadicks that the cancer was "one hundred percent in Kirt's blood stream." The doctors recommended chemotherapy, but Kirt made the final decision not to go that route. He told the doctors that he would go home and live out whatever life he had left without any further treatments. One thing that the doctors didn't tell the family until a little later was that they estimated he had no more than two months to live.

"I just couldn't understand it," Kirt says, reflecting on his feelings as the full weight of his condition sank in. "Here I was, only sixteen years old. I wondered why a kid like me would have to go through something like this. And it just blew my mom and dad out of the water. They couldn't believe it."

Sue and Ross Hadick and their four children attended a Pentecostal church near their home, and all had become committed Christians before Kirt was struck with cancer. But even with this personal introduction to the Kingdom of God, they felt completely unprepared to reach out for the miracle they knew they needed for Kirt.

"Before this crisis hit, I believed everything I'd heard my pastor preach about healing," Sue recalls. "I'd read great books on healing testimonies from some of the godliest men that ever lived. I'd even been privileged to see miracles happen. But if you walked up to me and said, 'Sue, give me five Scriptures on healing,' I'd have been at a loss. I personally had nothing 'hid in my heart' to stand against the enemy who had come in like a flood. [See Psalm 119:11.] I simply had not memorized the healing Word, so it could go from head to heart and spirit."

In effect, what Sue was saying was that it's important to know what the Bible says about miracles before we can know what our potential is to ask for them. This knowledge of the Scriptures is an essential prerequisite for a growing faith; and faith, of course, is a necessary element if one's life is to be filled with supernatural power.

Because of the fast deterioration in Kirt's physical condition, the Hadick family knew they would have to act quickly if they hoped to see a miracle before he died. So they crammed a lifetime's knowledge and experience of miracles into just a few weeks.

Sue plunged into the Scriptures, and by studying the miracles of Jesus in the Gospels she soon found that God honors faith. She said the only thing she could find in the New Testament that hindered Jesus from performing miracles was unbelief on the part of the people. So she and her family decided to get rid of all their unbelief and replace it with faith strong enough to stake their lives on.

In describing this process of building up their faith, Sue says, "We certainly were *willing* to have Kirt healed. Since 'faith comes by hearing and hearing by the Word of God,' we began by trying to increase our faith and not hindering Jesus through unbelief."

The Hadick family also learned to accept reality as what God wanted and not necessarily what human beings perceived as the "facts" in a particular situation. "Faith can be the exact opposite of fact," Sue noted. "Fact may not be what we see, feel, and hear. Jesus laid out a different principle for us—to walk by faith, not by sight."

Even though the facts that the doctors presented pointed toward Kirt's death, the Bible indicated he could be healed. So despite the fact that they didn't know where it might lead them, the Hadicks accepted the Bible as authority. And they began to use these spiritual "tools" which they found in the Scriptures.

> • *They memorized verses of Scripture and listened to tapes that taught biblical principles of healing.* "We had wonderful Christian friends who gave us the tapes, and I began memorizing Scriptures constantly," Sue said. "Verses were taped on the refrigerator and the mirrors in our home. I'd even take the tape recorder into the bathroom while I bathed. Extreme? yes, but so was the

situation. We had a boy who was dying fast, and the enemy had set the battle lines."

· *They began to "claim" God's promises.* Specifically, they believed that God would deliver on His promise in Proverbs 3:1–2 that if they "would not forget His Word and let their hearts keep His commandment," that would mean "length of days and years of life" for Kirt.

· *Others prayed and fasted for Kirt.* "Our pastor called [those in the] church to fast and pray and seek God for a miracle," Sue remembers. Also, another pastor brought a group of young people to visit and encourage Kirt, and they prayed for a miraculous healing. Before long, many others had joined in the powerful stream of prayer.

· *They rebuked Satan.* Sue came to realize that in Kirt's disease, they were confronting the ultimate enemy of good health, Satan, who "comes only to steal and kill and destroy." (John 10:10) So they specifically rebuked him in the name of Jesus.

With all this spiritual power being exerted around him, Kirt responded with a life-style that exuded faith. A week after he got home from the hospital, he returned to school, bandages and all, even though his parents had arranged to have him tutored at home.

Also, Kirt continued to refuse the opportunity for chemotherapy, even though he was told the treatments might lengthen his life somewhat. "If I was only going to have a limited period of time left on this earth, I didn't want to spend it getting doses of drugs which would cause me to be sick, lose my hair, and suffer bone deterioration," he said. "So I said, 'Lord God, this is it! I've got all of my apples in one basket. I'm going to believe in you and, if this doesn't cut it, then there's going to be no tomorrow.'"

At the same time that Kirt made this decision, he also made a commitment that "from here on, I'm going to go about like I'm healed." And he did just that. He went surfing and camping. He finished high school and then business college. He started working while he was in college and has continued to work. He recently got married and has been pronounced able to have children.

What about the two months he was given to live? Obviously, he's still alive and going strong! What about the cancer? Tests now show there is no cancer in his body.

The explanation? I'd say it's obvious, wouldn't you?

Believe and Receive—or Doubt and Do Without!

Ann Fieldman of Chicago knows the joy of having two children, ten grandchildren, and four great-grandchildren. She seemed to have everything going for her until February 1977, when she went to the doctor with a swollen left leg and lumps in the groin, which made it difficult to walk.

"It was also very painful," she recalls. "I thought the doctor would tell me to stay off my feet for a while and just rest. But that was not the case."

When the physician examined her, he was alarmed enough to have Ann admitted to a nearby hospital to try to find out what was causing her problem. After three days of tests, another lump appeared in her groin, and a biopsy was performed.

A few days later, the doctor, who shared Ann's Christian faith, returned to her hospital room to tell her the results. "He took my hand and we prayed," she says. "Then he told me his news was not good: The lump was malignant."

Specifically, he told her she had "malignant lymphoma, histiolymphocytic-type, Stage Four."

She asked, "When will it get to Stage Five?"

"There is no Stage Five," he replied, and then he waited for the despondent reaction that most of his patients would give.

But Ann didn't react with fear and discouragement. Instead, she said, "No Stage Five. But God can heal me! Nothing is impossible, no matter what the stage." Even as the doctor described in more detail the seriousness of her problem, she says, "I felt no qualms about the cancer being terminal."

But then the doctors decided she should undergo a series of twenty radioactive-cobalt therapy treatments in her groin and right leg, where the thigh bone, from the knee to the hip, was deteriorating from cancer.

In discussing the terrible ordeal of these treatments, Ann said, "My stomach became so large and distended I looked as though I were ready to have a child. I had such enormous tumors under my arms that I couldn't put my arms down. My neck was swollen, twice the size of my legs . . . and so it went from head to foot. But the cancer was spreading so rapidly they didn't know what to do."

Because the cobalt treatments hadn't been effective enough to stop the rampaging cancer, the doctors resorted to their last hope—chemotherapy. "After four chemotherapy treatments, I lost all of my hair; I lost about thirty-five pounds; and I developed ulcerated sores in my mouth and nose, and on my face."

In addition, she could no longer walk. She had to have her fifth and sixth treatments as an outpatient in a wheelchair. Finally, on the day of her scheduled seventh chemotherapy treatment, Ann managed to get up the strength to say she'd had enough. She says the Holy Spirit sort of "nudged" her, and when the doctor reached for the phone to call for the drugs, she said, "Don't call—I'm not going to take any more."

"Why, you need these treatments!" the doctor replied. "I can't be responsible for you if you don't take them."

"Good!" Ann answered. "The Lord will take over now." But she did agree to come back every two weeks for blood tests so that the doctor could determine whether the cancer had spread.

Ann says that when she arrived at her home, she found she accepted fully Jesus' statement "All things are possible to him who believes." (Mark 9:23) But she also proceeded to follow these seven "faith strategies," which helped to usher the healing power of God into her life.

1. She continuously expected Jesus to heal her. Although Ann had been through a variety of accepted medical treatments for cancer, in her heart she always saw Jesus as the healer. Medical science might be employed to help, but Ann didn't depend primarily on doctors, therapy, or operations.

One practical way she went about this was that she always "kept my eye on Jesus," as she puts it. She focused on Him in her mind and refused to allow distractions and doubts to enter her thinking. As a result, she was never upset or discouraged at any time by her illness.

"That's what brings victory in any problem," she says.

Also, since she possessed a *constant* expectation of the healing power of God, Ann was prepared spiritually and emotionally to hang on for as long as it might take for her to be healed.

2. She "claimed" the promises of Scripture. As Ann read the Bible, she particularly studied and memorized verses pertaining to healing and claimed them for herself. In other words, she believed that they should apply to her just as they applied to various people in the Old and New Testaments. Many others have found that memorizing passages of the Bible and then repeating them regularly can enhance their belief in God's power and make His promises come alive. This is the kind of spiritual environment in which miracles like healing often take place.

3. Ann talked regularly with God. She had a "walking and talking" relationship with the Lord. Or as she says, "Jesus spoke to me, and I spoke to Him. We had a running conversation."

By talking with God, Ann means that she regularly engaged in person-to-person communication with Him. She asked God questions and honestly laid out her concerns before Him, either audibly or silently. She also stayed attuned to God by reading the Bible.

To get a reply, she simply waited until she heard an answer from Him in her heart. God's constant presence with us, which we call the Holy Spirit, was the channel through which these communications came. Sometimes the response was immediate; at other times, she had to wait patiently; but the response always came.

On many occasions, of course, God will initiate the communication Himself. In any case, it's always important to be ready to listen for a word from Him. And that's the approach Ann consistently took, even during the darkest hours of her illness.

4. She asked Jesus to confirm His healing. It may seem strange to assume that you are being healed, even as your body deteriorates visibly before your eyes. But that's exactly what Ann did. And she didn't hesitate to ask God for some signals that would confirm the way He was working in her.

"Dear Jesus, I'm so sick and the pain is almost unbearable," she prayed. "But I know that you're healing me. What I need is a passage from your Word to comfort me." Then she waited and listened with her heart.

Finally, Ann sensed He was telling her, "Read John 11:4." She quickly went to get her Bible, and when she found that verse in her Bible, she began to cry with joy and relief. For the passage read: "This sickness is not unto death, but for the glory of God; that the Son may be glorified thereby."

4. Ann rebuked Satan. After Ann stopped taking chemotherapy treatments, she had four attacks of "excruciating pain in the breastbone." The pain was strong enough to cause her to lose consciousness. Each time this happened, she was taken to the hospital by ambulance, but the doctors could find no special reason for the pain. So Ann decided to check with God in prayer to find out what to do.

"As I read the Bible and prayed and meditated during the next few days," she said, "I came to the conclusion that since there was no medical explanation, it had to be the devil attacking me, trying to make me believe that I was not really being healed."

Soon after she had this insight, the severe chest pains came again, and her husband reached for the phone to call the doctor and an ambulance. But Ann stopped him.

"Don't call," she said. "I'm not going to the hospital!"

Then she told her husband that she was convinced the devil was attacking her and that she believed strongly Jesus had given her the power to do something about it. In retrospect, she knows now that her husband, looking at her in such a weakened condition, must have found it hard to believe she had power of any kind. She weighed only eighty-four pounds, she was bald, she was unable to walk, and she was racked by sores. But he reluctantly let her have her way—at least for the time being.

Ann knew that Jesus had rebuked Satan, his demons, and illnesses—such as the fever that had attacked Peter's mother-in-law in Luke 4:38–39. She also knew that there was tremendous power in invoking the name of Jesus—not in any magical sense, but in the sense of relying completely on the person of Jesus and the power inherent in Him. (See Acts 16:18 for Paul's use of Jesus' name.)

So she marshaled all her inner strength and said, "I rebuke you, Satan! I command you and your foul spirit of pain and disease to leave my body—in the name of Jesus!"

The pain left immediately after she uttered these words, and it hasn't returned. Her husband was so surprised that he threw his arms in the air and praised God along with her.

6. Ann took a long-term approach to building up her faith. Ann had worked at building up a strong faith even before the cancer struck. But she also continued to pursue the major sources of spiritual growth, such as Bible study, prayer, and fellowship with other Christians after her illness had incapacitated her.

Moreover, she filled her mind with her possibilities in God by spending some of her spare time watching Christian television programs, such as our *700 Club*. And she followed the basic Principle of Reciprocity, which I've mentioned elsewhere in this book. Despite her suffering, she faithfully gave to God's work. Undoubtedly, God honored this practice.

In other words, Ann was in a better position to receive after she had demonstrated her own generosity. Of course, the motive here can't be a matter of giving in order to get something.

The true biblical approach is to give without any worry about a return—yet with a knowledge that God has promised He will respond. There is a universal law. Jesus expressed it as "Give and it will be given to you." Expressed in physics it is "For every action there is an equal and opposite reaction." In the spiritual world, if you send out kindness, you get back kindness. If you send out hate, you get back hate. If you give, it is given to you—sometimes by people, and sometimes by God.

The prophet Malachi exhorted the people of his day to "prove Me [God] with your tithes and offerings" in order to see that God "would open you the windows of heaven and pour you out a blessing that there shall not be room enough to receive it." The "blessings" can be financial, they can be spiritual, and undoubtedly they can be, as in the case of Ann, related to physical health.

7. Finally, Ann helped herself.   Just as she had exhausted the medical solutions to her problem, she also paid close attention to the way she was living after she stopped medical treatments. For example, she started to improve her nutrition by taking vitamins and drinking lots of fresh fruit and vegetable juices. Then she waited expectantly for God to act—and His response soon came in a dramatic series of events:

- First of all, the sores in her mouth and nose began to disappear.
- By Easter of 1978, just a little more than a year after she had discovered she had cancer, she had gained back fifty of the pounds she had lost. To celebrate, she took the entire family out for Easter dinner.
- By the summer of 1978, her hair grew in—and as a bonus, it came in curly!

There were many other beneficial changes as well: When the cancer in Ann's body was at its worst, her thigh bone got wafer thin so that it tended to crumble under even the slightest pressure.

"Jesus did a creative miracle on that leg," she says. "Now I have a new bone in place of the cancerous one." As a result, she soon got rid of her wheelchair for good.

All this healing has taken place despite the fact, Ann says, that she has had no medication for cancer since she stopped taking those chemotherapy treatments in 1977. Her hospital report, which is contained in our files at *The 700 Club* and is dated January 2, 1980, says: "Past history revealed malignant lymphoma, non-Hodgkins type, Stage IV, three years ago, without any recurrence after years of follow-up."

Ann's antidote to cancer can be stated rather simply. She puts it this way: "I don't know what to say to anyone except to believe and receive—or doubt and do without!"

"Let the Little Children Come to Me. . . ."

Carole and Larry Baumgardner of Macomb, Illinois, seemed to have everything—three healthy children, a beautiful home, and a prosperous real-estate agency. They were doing well financially and looked forward to a bright future. But then, it seemed that the light in their lives would be snuffed out.

In November 1979 they discovered that their oldest son, five-year-old Tyson, had a massive, malignant brain tumor. The doctors could remove only about half of the tumor surgically because it was growing with the brain, and they didn't want to risk removing any brain tissue.

"He was critically ill," one of the nurses said. "The doctors told his parents it was a terminal tumor. They gave him six months to a year to live."

The Baumgardners were totally devastated. It seemed "like the end of the world." Little Ty underwent radiation treatment, which the doctors thought might retard the growth of the tumor, but they weren't very hopeful. It seemed unlikely that the radiation could actually destroy the tumor because of the serious type of malignancy, which was called "3rd ventricular astrocytoma."

Because the doctors weren't able to remove all the tumor, the passageways between the brain ventricles—or cavities containing important fluids—were blocked. "In order to get the ventricles communicating with one another, Ty underwent another surgery to place a shunt in his head," Carole recalls. "This was a tube that ran from his brain into his heart to circulate his brain fluid."

Ty went home after this, but then he became quite sick, and his parents had to take him back to the hospital. There he underwent several brain taps to drain the fluid from his brain. The situation quickly deteriorated.

"The doctors couldn't get Ty back into balance," Carole says. "One day, one of the doctors came into the hospital room and took my husband, Larry, aside and told him there was nothing more they could do for Ty."

By this time, Ty had dropped from fifty-four pounds down to thirty-three. The little fellow was pretty much skin and bones. "The thought of losing a child is, I think, the worst feeling you can ever go through," Larry says.

When the doctors told Larry that there was nothing more they could do, Larry went over to his son and sat down next to him. Ty was sleeping, in a state of total weakness.

Everything seemed lost. But then something quite amazing happened. As Larry puts it, the Lord spoke to him, saying, "The doctors have done all they can do. Now I'm going to do what only I can do."

"It was at that moment that I knew Ty would live," Larry says.

"We had complete faith and peace and knew that Ty was healed," adds Carole.

The Baumgardners, who had become committed Christians some time before, sensed their communication with God was completely open. So Larry just accepted what the Lord had told him—and both parents somehow knew down deep inside themselves, from that time on, that their son would be completely healed.

Soon afterward, when young Tyson returned to his room after one of his CAT scans, he told his parents that Jesus had actually met with him. He said he didn't see Jesus—but he had *heard* him. "Jesus said he'd heal me," Ty said simply.

His parents knew right away that this revelation had really come from Jesus because Ty had never mentioned anything like this on his own before. They felt their son's experience confirmed what they had already been told themselves.

"Our spirits soared because it was one of the many things the Lord did to show us along the way that Ty would not only recover, but he would be healed." Carole said.

But Tyson's condition didn't improve; it got worse.

In the spring of 1980, Carole and Larry noticed that the boy's vision was failing rapidly. A neuroophthalmologist who examined him found that Ty's optic nerves had apparently been permanently damaged by pressure from the growing brain tumor. Finally, Ty became legally blind, with 20/800 vision.

But even this additional disaster wasn't enough to shake the Baumgardners' faith. Carol said, "We kept our faith, and we continually 'confessed with our mouth' [Romans 10:9–10] that 'in the name of Jesus, Ty sees and Ty is healed.'"

She explains their attitude this way: "Larry and I knew that Ty was healed, and we would not accept in our hearts the diagnosis of blindness. We knew that 'in the name of Jesus' he *could* see." In fact, Larry and Carole went so far as to pray that Ty would be able to attend kindergarten in the fall—as a normal student.

Sure enough, against all medical predictions, Tyson began to improve.

First of all, his vision got better. His parents noticed that he was watching television, even though he was supposed to be legally blind. So they had him tested, and the doctor found that he had 20/400 vision instead of the 20/800 that had been recorded a few months earlier.

So Ty did indeed enter kindergarten in the fall just like other kids his age. During the first few months of classes, his vision seemed to continue to improve. To check it out, the Baumgardners took him to the doctor again in December 1980. This time, it was 20/50 in one eye and 20/40 in the other. A year later, his eyes became almost normal—20/20 close up, and 20/30 to 20/40 at a distance.

Larry said that a CAT scan taken in December 1981 was completely clear—there was not even any scar tissue inside his brain where the surgeries had been performed. Also, radiation treatments were supposed to have harmed Ty's pituitary gland, which controls growth. But further tests have shown no abnormalities or visible signs of damage. Moreover, the boy is growing taller regularly, without any growth hormones or medication.

As his parents had prayed and as they had expected, Tyson now goes to school and leads a completely normal life.

"God was with us every step of the way," Carole now says. "The experience has changed our lives. Many of our family members have come to know the Lord. Those around us have been made aware there is a living God who loves us. . . . Just looking at Ty now is a testimony in itself. Ty loves the Lord with all of his heart and he knows it was only because of Him and His love that he is healed today."

The Baumgardners conclude: "There is no explanation for it all, except God."

The Power in the Simple Act of Asking

Randy and Debbie Shesto were newlyweds from Milwaukee, Wisconsin. They had been married only about a year, and they were still savoring their budding romance and the prospects of a long and happy relationship when their dreams were suddenly shattered.

Randy, just twenty-one years old at the time, began to feel a pain in his abdomen. He went in for a checkup, and his doctor sent him on to a hospital for tests. Exploratory surgery was performed, and at first the physicians thought it was the appendix and then some problem with the bowels. They found nothing, however, and soon he was released from the hospital.

But the pain persisted.

At this point, his doctors told Randy, "It's all in your head." So he and Debbie, who was in nursing school, sought therapy with a psychologist.

Unfortunately, this counseling didn't help either, and the pain got so bad that Randy checked himself into a hospital once again. This time, the doctors made a disturbing discovery: Tests and X rays showed a mass approximately seven centimeters in diameter in his abdomen. The diagnosis: choriocarcinoma, a deadly cancer often found in males.

"My doctor told me that without treatment, I would be dead in two months," Randy said. "With treatment, I would possibly live a year, but I would be pretty well doped up all the time because of the pain. What a choice! My family talked me into taking the treatments."

Randy started with chemotherapy, which brought on violent bouts with nausea and vomiting. As a result, he lost 135 pounds and all his hair. After about eight months of chemotherapy, the doctors told him that his blood tests showed the cancer was almost gone, and so they suggested that they perform another operation and try to remove the rest with surgery.

Unfortunately, the doctors had been a little optimistic. He was under the knife for twelve hours, and the surgeons found he was filled with tumor from his diaphragm to his pelvis. The surgeons removed one kidney during the operation, but there was no way they could clean the malignancy completely out of his system. As a result, they put him back on chemotherapy.

But after two more treatments, he decided to quit. "By this time, I was yellow—not with a slight tint, but yellow," he says. "Even the whites of my eyes were yellow. I had weighed two hundred and four pounds before the cancer, but now I was down to one hundred and five—and still dropping. I believed I wouldn't live much longer."

But he still wasn't willing to give up. He even went to Florida to try the controversial Laetrile treatments and a vegetarian diet. As a matter of fact, after sticking with this regimen for several months, he did start feeling better. But still, he says, he knew he was dying and finally he gave up hope.

During these many months of pain and anguish, Randy turned away from God. He had been taught that it was God's will that some must suffer. In one church he had attended, he was even told that "God was not healing like he used to—and that my poor health was His will."

Thinking that God wouldn't help him—even that it was God's will for him to be in this condition—made him bitter and angry. But then he heard other people say that God can still heal people of terminal illnesses—right now, in the twentieth century. And he began to investigate that claim.

At the urging of a friend's mother, Randy tuned in to our *700 Club* television program. As he watched it every day for a week, he says, "I realized that the age of miracles is not over and that God is still healing people."

He heard increasing numbers of Christians say that poor health is not God's will. And he saw very ordinary people telling how they had been healed of a wide variety of maladies. But Randy was still deeply depressed and constantly felt tired. He really couldn't see that all the miracle stories he was hearing applied to him.

Then, in a final act of desperation, he decided to give these claims a try. He asked God either to take his life and let him die, or to heal him. He really wanted to live, but it took all the boldness and faith he could muster just to make this simple request.

Sometimes, the keys that God has given us to open the doors to His miracle kingdom seem deceptively simple. This was the case with Randy Shesto's simple act of asking. After he made this request, he says, "God answered me and told me I was healed! He spoke to me in my spirit and, at that instant, I *knew* beyond a shadow of a doubt that I was healed. I was up all night rejoicing!"

So Randy found that God was not only approachable but also that He had been there all the time, just waiting to be asked. Or as it says in Luke 11:9: "Ask and it will be given to you. . . ."

The next morning, Randy told Debbie he had been healed. Her reaction? "I thought the cancer had gone to his brain," she says. As a matter of fact, during the days that followed, she had little reason to change this opinion.

Randy's pain intensified, and if anything, his health seemed to be going further downhill. But he held on to the promise he had heard from God, and he continued to believe that he was being healed. Then God spoke to him again: "It's the Devil causing the pain."

Randy was a little disconcerted at this message because, as he said later, "I'd never known that you could rebuke Satan and claim God's healing power." But he did just that: He rebuked Satan's presence in his body. Then he woke up one morning about a week later, and the pain had disappeared.

At the same time that God informed Randy of the healing, He gave him the empowering experience known to the early Christians. (See Acts 2:4.) Randy was baptized with the Holy Spirit. As a result, Randy became a different person—overnight. As Debbie remembers it, the long months of suffering had strained their marriage nearly to the point of divorce.

"It was almost impossible living with Randy when he was resigned to death," Debbie recalls. "But after he asked God for healing, he changed in every way."

Soon, new blood tests were performed and "they revealed normal readings for the first time in two years," Randy says. He also started gaining weight, and now he weighs two hundred fifteen pounds—normal for his six-foot-three-inch frame.

After this miraculous healing and the spiritual growth that they experienced along with it, the Shestos are living a completely new life. The once skeptical Randy has done some work in Christian counseling, attended Bible college, and begun a new church in Milwaukee called The Word Center. Randy also hosts a weekly radio program on which he tells his listeners about the miracle-working God he serves.

It's amazing, isn't it, what incredible things can arise from a simple act like asking God to bring His power into our lives?

But these supernatural healings are only an introduction to the way miracles can change your life. There are many, many other ways that God can intervene in the natural order He has established. What I'm referring to—and what I want to consider in the next chapter—is the miraculous manner in which God can rescue those faced with sure and terrifying disaster.

CHAPTER FOUR

The Power to Control Events That Are Out of Control

In a sense, every answer to prayer—indeed, every subtle nudge God gives us—is a miracle because it's an intervention by the supernatural into our three-dimensional, natural realm. Still, there's a more precise sense in which the term *miracle* is used in the Bible. A number of words are used to refer to miraculous happenings in the Old and New Testaments, but they have several common threads that set them apart from other works of God in our lives:*

> • *They are different from most other happenings, and their distinctiveness provokes wonder in those who ob-*

*See *The New Bible Dictionary*, J. D. Douglas, ed. (Grand Rapids, Mich.: Eerdmans Publishing Co., 1962), pp. 828–29.

serve them. For example, in his song commemorating the parting of the Red Sea and the destruction of Pharaoh's army, Moses exclaims: "Who is like thee, O Lord, among the gods . . . terrible in glorious deeds, doing wonders?" (Exodus 15:11)

- *They involve expressions of great might and power.* In this regard, Jesus said about the city of Capernaum, "If the mighty works done in you had been done in Sodom, it would have remained until this day." (Matthew 11:23) He was apparently referring back to such miracles as His healing of a centurion's paralyzed servant even when He was separated from the servant by a great distance; the healing of Peter's mother-in-law who had been stricken with a "high fever"; the casting out of demons, and the calming of a great storm on the Sea of Galilee. (See Matthew 8:5ff; Luke 4:31ff.)

- *They communicate something deeply meaningful or spiritually significant.* King Darius, for instance, who was quite impressed with how Daniel survived the lions' den, wrote this to his subjects: "I make a decree, that in all my royal dominion men tremble and fear before the God of Daniel. . . . He delivers and rescues, he works signs and wonders in heaven and on earth, he who has saved Daniel from the power of the lions." (Daniel 6:25–27)

Clearly, then, miracles are extraordinary, amazing events which are caused by the direct action of God in our human affairs and which typically inspire a reaction of great wonder. Moreover, in many cases these happenings run entirely contrary to ordinary human expectations, and they may accomplish last-ditch, life-saving results for the individuals involved.

Now, let's turn to some concrete illustrations. The two highly unusual events that follow show how the powerful forces of God's invisible kingdom can intervene to achieve a last-minute rescue—even in those seemingly hopeless situations that have careened totally out of control.

A Divine Flying Lesson

On a cold, windy January day, Edmund Gravely coaxed his wife, Janice, out of their cozy home in Rocky Mount, North Carolina, and the two of them headed for the local airport.

Edmund, who at sixty-one was an avid amateur pilot, had just learned that a new Ventus-b sailplane, which he had ordered from Europe, had arrived in Statesboro, Georgia. Too impatient to wait for the delivery to be made in North Carolina, he persuaded his sixty-year-old wife to join him for a three-hour spin down to Statesboro in their single-engine silver Mooney 20.

Janice was a little reluctant at first. After all, the temperature was down to 9 degrees Fahrenheit, with a wind-chill factor of −36. But her husband's enthusiasm finally convinced her. And besides, the cabin of the plane quickly became so warm and comfortable that she shed her heavy coat and tossed it on the backseat.

Although the trip was a bit of a lark for the Gravelys, they quickly discovered a somewhat sobering factor: Wind gusts had been reported up to thirty-two miles per hour, and that could create some problems in the air. But the plane they were flying was heavier and better equipped than the one they had previously owned, so they weren't really too concerned.

As a young man, Edmund had been a naval aviator, and he had continued to keep up his flying skills as a civilian. The sailplane was something he had developed a recent interest in, just as a hobby. As they flew south that day, it became evident that the piloting demands were routine for an expert aviator like Edmund. The plane bounced through the cold headwinds much as a water skier skips across a boat's wake—it was fun and provided a little variety, without being too demanding. Janice, who was also thoroughly relaxed, divided her time between some tatting she had brought along and gazing over the pretty countryside below them.

"There's Fayetteville!" Edmund yelled above the cabin noise as he pointed toward some clusters of buildings on the ground. He then indicated the spot on the map in his wife's lap. A few minutes later, he leaned to his right, as if to check the map.

"What are you looking at, honey?" Janet asked. But Edmund didn't answer. She looked up at him, and to her horror, she saw that he was unconscious. When she checked more closely, it became evident that he wasn't even breathing. Uncertain what the problem was but fearing the worst, she pushed him straight up in his seat and leaned his head back in an effort to help him breathe. But he still didn't respond. In fact, when she checked more closely, she found his heart wasn't beating. Edmund had never had any heart trouble before, but apparently his problem now was a massive heart attack—one that had taken his life.

Janet continued to apply what first aid she could in a frantic attempt to revive her husband—and she prayed more fervently than she could ever remember praying in the past. "He was easy to pray for because he was a man of faith," she says. "And God had healed him of many things through prayer. I prayed for him like I'd never prayed for anybody in my life."

But finally, Janet realized there was nothing else she could do for him, and so she sat back, determined to control her panic and grief. Her main goal now was to get the plane down safely and perhaps get Edmund to a hospital emergency room. First she removed her husband's glasses, which were attached to a radio receiver and transmitter, and placed them on her head. Although the plane had dual controls, he was the only one with radio equipment.

Janice used the microphone connected to the glasses to send out an urgent distress call: "Help, help! Won't somebody help me? My pilot is unconscious!"

She repeated these words over and over, but didn't think to identify the plane or give her location. Failing to receive a reply, she switched channels and tried again. But lacking experience in handling the radio equipment, she somehow so detuned the system that it was impossible for her to send or receive any messages. As a result, there was absolutely no chance of her getting help from another plane or from anyone on the ground. Now, whatever happened would be up to Janice—and to God.

Fortunately, the plane was equipped with a wing leveler, a device that automatically keeps a craft balanced evenly in the air. As a result, the Mooney had been flying all right by itself, despite the turmoil in the cockpit. But now the time had come for Janice to try to get back to the ground, and she had no idea where to start. Although Edmund had been qualified as a flight instructor, she had never bothered to learn a thing about flying.

Before attempting the strange controls, Janet sat back again to pray—and this time it was praise that came from her lips. Even though she was in great danger, she realized she had something to be thankful for: The Mooney, which the Gravelys had owned for only about a month, was equipped with a wing leveler while their previous plane had not had this device. In other words, if Edmund had experienced this attack just a few weeks before, the old plane wouldn't have stayed steady, flying by itself, and a crash would have been likely almost immediately.

So Janice praised God that she was in this particular plane and that, for however long, at least she was still flying.

Now she began to check the instruments. Having flown with her husband enough to know a few basic things, she saw that they were flying much higher than usual. Apparently Edmund had moved to a higher altitude to avoid some of the air pockets. The altimeter read 6,000 feet. The compass and air-speed indicator showed they were going south at about 180 miles per hour.

But that was all she learned from the instrument panel. And certainly she had no idea about how to fly or land the plane. So once again, she prayed: "Lord, what am I doing up here? I need to get down and get some help for Edmund!"

Then, as Janice began to focus more on God, she was suddenly gripped by a feeling of extraordinary peace. It was something that seemed to "come all over" her. As she puts it, "Peace seemed to fill the cockpit of the plane. It just flooded out of God and into the cabin." Even as the plane occasionally hit extremely rough spots, Janice stayed calm and assured. "Can you imagine peace in such a situation—when the air was so turbulent it almost threw us around in the cabin?" Janice asks. Yet the peace stayed with her—and at the same time, she began to sense some inner answers to the questions she was putting to God.

When she had asked, "Lord, what am I doing up here?," she was inquiring, in part, why they had drifted to such a relatively high altitude for their small plane. At that point, the feeling of peace that came upon her was accompanied by a thought that she knew could only come from God: "You're at six thousand feet to give you more time to become acquainted with this airplane."

So she immediately began checking the plane, trying to remember what Edmund had done. She discovered there were thirteen dials and thirty-five switches on the instrument panel, but they were totally unfamiliar—except for the altimeter, airspeed indicator, and compass.

Then she found a set of written directions she had never seen before: "To go north, fly 350—fly south 170." These numbers apparently referred to the degree headings on the compass that would cause the plane to go due north or south. She knew from the compass reading that now they were heading just about due south. She now had to decide whether to keep heading in that direction—which involved a lot of unfamiliar territory—or to try to turn the plane around and head back toward the more familiar territory of North Carolina.

After thinking and praying about the situation for a few moments, she decided to turn the plane around and head north. That way, she might find the Rocky Mount airport—or at least some familiar ground where she could crash-land.

So she grabbed the yoke—the steering wheel–like lever in front of her—and began to turn it to the right, as she had seen Edmund do on many occasions. Edmund always seemed to perform this task with ease, but the action took all Janice's strength because the automatic wing leveler was still on and worked against her. Still, little by little, as she fought against the leveler, the plane gradually swung around—until she was close to a northward heading on the compass. The plane continued flying at too high an altitude, however, so Janice tried pushing forward—again, as she had observed her husband do. Once more, it was hard work because of the leveler. But by pushing with all her strength, Janice found she could overcome the device for short periods of time and move the plane lower and lower toward the ground.

In between these wrestling bouts with the wing leveler, she searched the horizon for the contours of the Rocky Mount airport or any other familiar site—but in vain. Apparently, even though she was heading in the right direction, the wind was blowing her off course.

Janice zoomed through the air for nearly two hours, and you might think that the constant pressure over such a long period would have caused her spirits, if not the plane itself, to come crashing down. But Janice had other resources. She sang hymns and praised God as she flew along.

"I got happy in the Lord," she says. "The situation was terrible, but I knew I was all right." Also, she knew there was nothing more she could do for Edmund at that point.

Although Janice kept looking for an airport, she found nothing that even resembled a landing strip. Finally, as she was nearing Henderson, North Carolina (though she had no idea at the time about her location), she decided she had better try to crash-land. So she picked a freshly plowed open field, which was surrounded by a forest near a road. No power lines were in sight—that was one of the prerequisites Janice had settled upon as she had been thinking and praying about her plight.

She applied steady pressure on the yoke and headed down toward her chosen landing site, where she knew she would have to belly in since she didn't know how to lower the landing gear. But then, unexpectedly, the plane ran out of gas and the engine quit abruptly on her. The stubby-winged plane began dropping "like a brick," well short of the clearing she had spotted.

"God decided I wasn't going to land in the field I'd picked," she says.

Instead, she touched down in a sparsely wooded area, which had been burned and reforested with saplings. As the Mooney barreled in at 130 mph, its momentum was broken as each thin young tree caught the wings or fuselage. Bit by bit, the forward motion of the craft slowed. Finally, Janet found herself sitting in the badly damaged craft on the edge of a dirt road, which separated her sparsely wooded landing field from the more open area she had originally chosen.

Gradually, the significance of what had happened dawned on her. As she looked across the more open site, she saw the solid woods that formed an impregnable wall on the other side. If she had actually landed where she had originally planned, the Mooney would have been going too fast to stop. It would have skidded pellmell across the open terrain and crashed violently into those big trees on the other side. There was no way Janice could have survived such an impact.

And what if the plane hadn't run out of gas in the air just before she landed? What if she had hit those heavy woods with plenty of extra gas in the tank? She shuddered to think of the fires and explosions that might have engulfed her.

Clearly, the God who had given her an incredible sense of peace and control up there in the air had stepped in at the last moment, when the situation had moved well beyond human analysis and control. The landing field that God had chosen—and the timely lack of gas—were the last, life-saving part of the miraculous, divine flying lesson that Janice Gravely had been given.

Of course, neither she nor the plane emerged from the accident completely unscathed. One tree tore the right wing and door off the craft. "I watched the tree hit the wing and then I just gave in," she says. "It was the most turbulence I'd ever been in. When we hit the bottom, it was absolutely the worst thing I'd ever gone through. But we stopped!"

She had kept her eyes shut tightly during most of the harrowing landing. But after the craft had ground to a halt, Janice recalls, she opened her eyes and was nearly blinded by an incredibly bright light. "It was the most brightness I'd ever seen—and I was alive!"

We may never know exactly what this brightness was. Perhaps it was merely a physical phenomenon resulting from the jolts Janice received during the landing. But it's also interesting to note that many profound spiritual experiences have been accompanied by an inexplicable, overwhelming light. To name just a few, there were:

- the conversion of the nineteenth-century evangelist and reformer Charles Finney;
- the conversion of the Apostle Paul (Acts 9);
- the transfiguration of Christ (Mark 9:2–8).

Whatever the light was, it signaled the culmination of Janice's unsettling flight—but not the end of the miracles that were to follow. After the light receded and the world returned to its normal colors, Janice slipped on her warm jacket. She then leaned over to Edmund, and said, "I'll be back in a minute, honey."

She intended to walk over to a nearby house, which she had spotted from the air, and get some help. But when she got out of the plane, she was surprised to find she couldn't stand up. She had suffered a broken pelvis and severe bruises from the crash, and was unable even to walk with a stick that she picked up near the wreckage. So she had to crawl.

Somehow, Janice managed to inch her way on both hands and one knee through thick underbrush and across a field. The trek covered about two hundred yards—and that wasn't so easy for a sixty-year-old woman who had just survived an airplane crash.

"It *was* a pretty long, bad crawl," she remembers. "But I never experienced too much difficulty as long as I kept my eyes on Jesus."

She kept repeating, "I can do all things through Christ who strengthens me." And God did strengthen her, for she finally made it to the house she had spotted. What's more, the house was occupied not by just anyone but by a nurse.

The nurse, Lovey Jones, first thought the wobbling, sagging woman on her doorstep was drunk. Janice was truly a terrible sight: Her hands were bloody from crawling, and she was so exhausted she had rested her head on Lovey's front steps. But the thing that made Lovey realize she was dealing with a sober, seriously injured person was the stream of words that kept pouring out of Janice's mouth—words of praise for God.

So Lovey Jones quickly got in touch with the nearest doctor and hospital. A rescue team checked the plane, but unfortunately, as Janice had feared from the beginning, Edmund was dead. He had apparently suffered a fatal heart attack in the air when he collapsed against her shoulder.

Janice was treated for a broken pelvis, four broken ribs, a punctured and collapsed lung, and several internal injuries. As a matter of fact, the doctors wanted to reinflate her lung, but Janice and her family and friends decided to try another approach first. Two groups prayed for her, and the doctors soon found that the lung was healing on its own. She was released from the hospital in ten days and was able to walk without a cane in a few weeks.

One fascinating little footnote to this story involves the Gravelys' son Edmund junior who was at work on the national news desk of *The New York Times* on the very night that his parents' plane went down. A United Press wire-service report about the crash caught his eye. It was in this way that he learned that his father was dead but that somehow, against all odds, his mother had survived the accident and been taken to a hospital.

"That's how I found out I had lost the man I most dearly loved and liked and respected," Edmund junior says. "But I also knew he died quickly, probably painlessly, never agonizing over the danger my mother was in. More than that, it was as if my mother had been raised from the dead."

Later, in assessing what had happened to his mother, Edmund junior said, "God was in control of events. Had mother found an airport, she would have crashed on concrete with sparks flying and gasoline burning. Had she made the plowed field she was aiming for, she would have bounced off into tall trees and probably died from the sudden stop. Or the plane would have exploded. As it was, she ran out of gas at exactly the right moment to come down in the only condition possible to survive."

Janice firmly believes that both her husband's death and her own miraculous escape from death were all part of God's plan for them: "There was nothing coincidental about anything that happened that day. God had it all in place."

To understand more fully the exact way that God "had it all in place" and how He set the stage for this miracle, it's necessary to go back a number of years and see how God prepared the Gravelys for the event.

Janice became a Christian in 1963.   Soon after she accepted Jesus as her Savior in 1963, Janice got into the habit of "praising the Lord." By this, she means that she regularly worshiped Him in private and public meetings, and she openly, verbally extolled His goodness and power in her own life and in the world at large. Also, the practice of genuine praise assumes that God has been given first place in our lives. That's the attitude that Janice expressed, and she grew steadily in her knowledge and love of Him.

The family had experienced a previous healing miracle. Janice's faith was strengthened considerably in the early 1970s when doctors diagnosed the Gravelys' younger daughter, Louise, as having acute lymphatic leukemia—which is usually fatal. But Louise was unexpectedly healed after Janice, the other family members, and members of their church prayed for the girl. So by the time that Janice faced the terror of the plane crash, her faith in God was solid.

Edmund later became a Christian. It was after his daughter Louise became seriously ill that Edmund also came to accept Jesus Christ as his Savior and Lord. As Edmund junior says, the burden of his sister's illness sent his father to his knees, "and he found real cleansing and strength in Christ." Janice describes her husband as being a very devout Christian during the last ten years of his life. During this period, he began to share his faith with anyone who expressed an interest in Jesus.

The four Gravely children made a commitment to Christ. The Gravelys' two sons and two daughters were all grown when their father died. But like their mother and father, they had become committed Christians before that tragedy, and this fact served as a great consolation in understanding and accepting Edmund senior's death.

In writing an account of his father's death, Edmund junior said, "He now sees face to face what we see in a glass darkly. I feel certain that from his new perspective he would want nothing more than for those who read of his death to know Him who rescues the perishing and saves the dying."

The family believed that God can use even the worst tragedy for the greatest good. God, of course, can do what He wants, regardless of the faith or expectations of any human being. But it's part of His scheme of things in the universe to involve men and women in His work—including miraculous work. One way that God brings us into the process of shaping history is to take the beliefs we have in His promises, show us how He fulfills those promises and then allow us to proclaim to the world how faithful He is.

In the case of the Gravelys, they believed the principle, stated so well in Romans 8:28: "And we know that in all things God works for the good of those who love him, who have been called according to his purpose." In other words, Janice was completely convinced that God would somehow use her husband's death to effect a broader purpose.

Specifically, she felt that Edmund was "picked by God for this signal honor" because he was well-known and respected, both in the United States and abroad. At the time of his death, he was president of the China-American Tobacco Company in Rocky Mount, North Carolina, president of the Chesapeake Storage Corporation in Richmond, Virginia, president of the Virginia Gazette, Inc., of Williamsburg, Virginia, and chairman of the board of directors of a local bank. It seemed to Janice that his prominence would make it more likely that reports of the circumstances of his death, including her miraculous escape, would be circulated widely.

Sure enough, the news media immediately picked up on the event. In the time since the crash occurred, the family's strong Christian faith has been reported extensively on radio and television, and in various newspapers and national magazines. Consequently, as the story continues to be told and retold, the work of God in the world is communicated in a dramatic and understandable way.

Of course, every member of the family misses Edmund senior deeply. But still, Janice concludes, "Had Edmund died in church, God would not have been as glorified."

In the last analysis, then, the story of this miracle is first the story of a family made spiritually resilient through a deep faith. But it's also an account of those who were prepared to tell others about the extraordinary supernatural channels through which God may act in our ordinary lives.

Some of these same elements are also present in another story of God's ability to work miracles in the air. But in this next case, the plane was not a pleasure craft but a supersonic fighter plane.

When God Moved Faster Than a Fighter Plane

"I trusted my airplane implicitly and explicitly," declares Lieutenant Colonel Kris Mineau, a solidly built, seasoned fighter pilot who safely flew one hundred missions over North Vietnam.

A graduate of the U.S. Air Force Academy, Mineau had complete faith in his F-4 Phantom II. In addition to being perhaps the nation's most versatile fighter bomber, the plane had been a mainstay of the air force operations in Vietnam. In some respects, the F-4 is the most successful supersonic fighter ever built. More than five thousand have been produced, and they are used by ten nations around the world. Powered by twin jet engines, the F-4 flies at two and a half times the speed of sound and can carry twelve thousand pounds of bombs and missiles.

Kris Mineau's rather disturbing adventure with his F-4—an adventure which brought him face to face with death—began in

Woodbridge, England, in March 1969. He and a navigator set out on a routine air-combat training mission. Kris immediately began to put the aircraft through its paces, and everything was going quite smoothly.

Then, toward the end of the flight, Kris rolled the plane into an upside-down position at 15,000 feet and started moving into an outside loop. But to his consternation, the cockpit flight controls instantly froze "full forward." This meant that the fighter, instead of swinging around and up in a loop, began to hurtle straight down toward the ground at 750 miles per hour. Kris was moving at a supersonic speed of more than 1,000 feet per second—and the velocity of his craft was accelerating. Most frightening of all, the angle and rate of descent meant that Kris had only ten seconds to rectify the malfunction before he plowed his own grave in the fast-approaching earth.

"I spent the first nine seconds pulling every trick out of my bag of lifelong experience as a pilot to make the aircraft respond," he recalls. "But it was all to no avail. The flight controls remained frozen, completely out of my control. They just wouldn't move."

This left Kris only about one second, one fleeting instant of time, for his last resort—ejection from the cockpit. So he pulled the handle of the ejection-seat mechanism, but nothing happened. His canopy was jammed. The navigator had already ejected, but Kris couldn't get free. The high technology that he had always trusted to make his chariot perform perfectly had somehow failed when he needed it most.

Even as I recount this terrifying ordeal, I realize it takes much more than a second or two for me to get the story across or for you to read it. But in moments of intense crisis, something seems to happen to time. It appears to slow down dramatically. Much more gets crammed into our minds, reactions, and memories than is possible in our more relaxed moments.

THE POWER TO CONTROL EVENTS

That seems to be what happened to Lieutenant Colonel Kris Mineau in that final second or two before impact. He was no longer the assured, self-sufficient captain of his ship. Instead, without warning, Kris had become a very frightened passenger on an aircraft that was making a one-way trip to eternity.

But then a chain of extraordinary events began to occur—a series of incredible happenings that, taken together, can only be understood in terms of some sort of outside, extradimensional intervention. There were five distinct extraordinary phases—or miracles, if you will—in this process, none of which can be adequately explained in ordinary terms.

Miracle #1. In the final split second before impact, Kris sensed his whole life passing before him, like scenes from a movie. Simultaneously, he called out to a God whom he said he "didn't even know." Also, he frantically pulled in vain at the handles that were supposed to eject him. In his panic and despair, he cried, "Please God, help me!"

Suddenly, the jammed canopy separated, and the ejection seat fired. But even though Kris was now in the open air, he was far from being safe. The chute needed two to three thousand feet of altitude to open—but he was only five hundred feet from the ground.

Miracle #2. Mathematically and technologically, there was no possible way for the parachute to open in less than three seconds. Yet it opened in less than half a second. To this day, no one, including Kris Mineau, knows how it happened. But because that parachute "decided" to operate, Kris made it to the ground alive. Still, he wasn't safely home yet.

Miracle #3. When Kris hit the ground, he was going much faster than he would have been if his chute had opened at a higher altitude. As a result, even though he lived, the impact caused him to suffer two broken arms, two broken legs, and various internal injuries. But he was conscious, and he could move his head—a good sign that his back and neck were still operating all right.

Nearby villagers saw his F-4 plow into the ground at 750 miles per hour, where it made a crater fifty feet across and fifty feet deep. Investigators found parts of the plane as far below the surface as seventy-five feet, and the largest piece that remained intact was a thirty-nine-foot engine.

The villagers also saw Kris come barreling down in his chute, and within half an hour, a British military helicopter had arrived to rush him to a local hospital. The first reaction of the medical authorities who examined him was amazement that he hadn't been totally dismembered. Other ejections at similar speeds and altitudes had resulted in brutal dismemberment by the supersonic wind-blasts and pressures.

But even though it was agreed that Kris shouldn't have survived, he still faced months of hospitalization, surgery, and traction. During this period, he had ample time to reflect on his accident and his incredible survival. Although he was not a religious person, the only explanation he could come up with was that his being alive was a miracle of God. This insight didn't motivate him to make any sort of commitment to God, however. Kris just acknowledged the divine intervention that he believed had saved him, and then, essentially unaffected, he turned back to his old ways.

Kris was medevaced (evacuated for medical purposes) in a full body cast to a U.S. Air Force base in Florida. He expected to get back on his feet without too much delay, and he was determined to do it his own way—by sheer grit and force of will. That's the way he had succeeded in everything he had tried in the past, and that was the way he would conquer this problem.

But things didn't prove to be quite that easy. After six months, his doctors told him that the bones had healed improperly and they would have to be rebroken. Kris had sustained a positive attitude up to this point. But the bad news made him feel as though he had gone through another crash—one that was more emotional and spiritual than physical.

It was during this down period, when he was flat on his back and his spirits were at their lowest ebb, that an air force chaplain paid a visit. The man also wore a set of pilot's wings, and that increased Kris's respect for him. They began to trade war stories, and for the first time in weeks, Kris began to enjoy himself. But then the chaplain dropped a bombshell: He asked Kris if he believed in Jesus Christ.

"That crazy chaplain had the nerve to ask me that!" Kris says. He certainly believed in the historical Jesus—that He was a great teacher who had lived and died in the first century. But he wasn't sure about anything more than that.

Still, the two men continued talking, and before long, Kris recalls, "It finally hit me like the proverbial ton of bricks. The chaplain said that Jesus even died for the North Vietnamese— and I cried like a baby. You see, at that time in my life, I thought the North Vietnamese were the worst people on earth. But now, I finally knew that the gospel was real and that Jesus had died for *my* sins, too."

At this moment, the self-sufficient, hot-dog pilot says he had a personal revelation of what Jesus had done for him on the cross—and "all the hurt, frustrations, and burdens were lifted from me."

Unfortunately, Kris didn't begin immediately to build on his new-found faith. He really didn't understand that he was supposed to do anything other than make this commitment. So he more or less stood still in his new spiritual life, and finally he "put the Lord on the shelf."

Despite his lack of attention to further spiritual development, good news about his injuries immediately followed his commitment. His medical situation improved, and after radical surgery, he was able to walk again to some extent. Although one leg was still in a cast and the other in a brace, and his arms had to be propped up with crutches, still, for the first time in what seemed to be ages, he could get around on his own feet.

Even as Kris underwent these procedures and experienced some improvement, he kept Christ at arm's length. He feared that if he got too serious with God, he might lose his career as a pilot. But clearly, his decision to "run from God," as he puts it, wasn't helping him improve very quickly. Although several of his limbs and injuries were mending, his left leg remained in a cast for months. The doctors even started talking about the possibility of another operation, and Kris began to wonder if the surgery would ever end.

Finally, he realized that if he was ever going to be cured completely, the healing would have to come from God—not merely from his own willpower or from medical expertise.

Miracle # 4.   Despite Kris's failure to take the initiative in his own spiritual development, God was still at work in his life. But the time was no longer appropriate for dramatic, quick miracles. Apparently God now decided to use a healing of the pilot's body as the means to heal his spirit. That is, He put Kris in a position where he grew and matured through a deepening of his faith. Here are some of the faith steps that Kris experienced:

Faith Step One: Kris found himself involved in in-depth encounters with committed Christians.   He and his wife, Lura, were living in base housing at MacDill Air Force Base in Florida, when they discovered that some of their neighbors were committed Christians.

"Just through normal backyard social contacts, we became acutely aware of the beliefs and convictions of these people," Kris says.

Their neighbors were joyful and stimulating, and Kris found himself drinking in the biblical information they furnished. "For the first time, I didn't want to talk about airplanes. I wanted to talk about God!" said Kris.

Faith Step Two: Kris made a firmer commitment of his life to Jesus. Kris quickly perceived that the difference between his life and theirs was that they had first totally committed their lives to Christ and then proceeded to build on that commitment. In a sense, they were really radical in their willingness to put God first in every aspect of their lives. But far from being a "bunch of fanatics," he says, they were personally attractive and fascinating to be around. So Kris concluded that the time had come for him to make the same sort of total commitment of his life.

"On a warm July night in 1970, I went to bed and decided to pray," he recalls. "I couldn't get on my knees [because of my injuries], so I lay in bed and said, 'God, I don't want to do the things Kris Mineau wants to do any longer. I want to do the things *you* want Kris Mineau to do.'"

Faith Step Three: Kris's entire being was filled with God's Spirit. Our closest contact with God in this three-dimensional world of ours is through His Holy Spirit, whom we can't see, smell or touch—but who is more real than the ground we walk on. The real power in a relationship with God comes from being filled and sustained by His Spirit, and that's the kind of experience Kris had next. Putting it as well as he can in ordinary human terms, he says, "Heaven came down, and glory filled my soul." Moreover, he was filled with "a warmth, love, and joy that were inexpressible."

This experience with the Spirit came on the heels of his decision to make a total commitment of his life to Christ, and that's typical of what many others have encountered. Acquiring the full power of God's Spirit in your life depends on completely turning your life over to God. It's a matter of explicitly asking Him to come into your deepest being and take over your goals, concerns, needs, and ambitions.

Faith Step Four: God "spoke" and promised healing. To be filled with the Spirit of God and to be led and instructed by God's Spirit should be a normal part of a Christian's life. God normally speaks to our inner being in a still, quiet way. However, there are times when He speaks in an audible voice. As with other miracles, a divine voice, vision, or appearance may be just an unusual expression of God's love to confirm an already developing faith, or it may be an added nudge that some people need to get started on the road to faith in the first place. Whatever the reason with Kris, as part of his commitment experience, he heard a "voice." Furthermore, he knew it was the voice of the Lord, who communicated this clear message:

"Welcome home, my prodigal son. I have waited for all eternity for you to make this decision. Trust in me, and your leg will be healed. For you, it will take time. But in that time, I will get you where I want you."

After these words, Kris fell into a deep sleep and he says that from the moment he woke the next morning, his life has never been the same.

Faith Step Five: He spent his convalescence studying the Bible. Despite his new spiritual strength, Kris's left leg just wouldn't heal immediately. Long visits to different hospitals became part of his routine. But he didn't waste the free time that he had.

"God saw to it that I had plenty of time to study His word [and thereby] make up for thirty years of ignorance," he explains. "Studying the Bible became like a two-year college crash course. The continued hospitalization was truly a blessing in disguise."

Kris's observations about the possible reason for the delay in his healing—to give him time to develop more fully spiritually—reminds me of the experience of the biblical character Zacharias, the father of John the Baptist. In the first chapter of the Gospel of Luke, Zacharias voices doubt that the angel Gabriel is really speaking the truth when he tells Zacharias that his elderly, barren wife, Elizabeth, will bear a son. The angel then proceeds to take away Zacharias's ability to speak, but it's restored nine months later, when John the Baptist is born.

When Zacharias gets his speech back, he's a completely different person: His first words are words of deep belief and blessing for God, rather than doubt. In effect, by suffering a severe physical disability, Zacharias seems to have been put on a nine-month retreat during his wife's pregnancy. The time he was forced to spend alone with God during that period seems to have been just the spiritual prescription he needed to develop a healthy faith.

Somewhat the same combination of spiritual and physical recuperation appears to have occurred with Kris Mineau. God gave him physical strength gradually. Three and a half years and ten operations after the accident, the doctors deemed his body clinically healed. But then there followed another year and a half of orthopedic braces.

Kris was assigned to a nonflying position in the air force, and he finished graduate school and became a math instructor at the Air Force Academy. Finally, he was able to leave behind all the orthopedic devices—the canes, crutches, and braces. The miraculous mending God had promised to Kris was finally completed. And most important, he had also made giant strides in his spiritual life. But still, Kris hadn't returned to full flying status, and that had been one of his main goals after the accident. The stage was set for the final great miracle in his life.

Miracle # 5. The story had gone out that Kris was washed up as a pilot, and for consolation he had turned to religion. But Kris had another view of the situation. He sensed that if he was to make the greatest impact for God in the air force, it would be important for him to get back to flying. So he went to the flight surgeon's office and began to take the steps that were necessary to accomplish this goal.

Because of the extent of his injuries and the length of time he had been grounded, Kris had to undergo extensive evaluations—much like the flight physicals for astronauts and test pilots. His case was unique: He had been written off as a hopeless invalid but was now claiming he was ready to return to his former status in the air. As a result, the decision in his case was referred to the Air Force Surgeon General for final determination.

On January 1, 1975, Kris received orders from the Chief of Staff of the Air Force confirming his return to flying status. He was immediately assigned to ground and academic training for F-4s. Finally, the big day came. When he got his orders, he found his takeoff time was 4:30 P.M. on Tuesday, March 25, 1975.

The time was especially significant because his accident had occurred at 4:30 P.M. on Tuesday, March 25, 1969. In other words, his return as a pilot took place exactly six years to the day and hour after his near-fatal accident. Not only that, when he picked up his aircraft number assignment, he found it was

Number 898—the same as the aircraft number he had been flying when his accident occurred!

"Thus, the Lord showed me how my life, which had been violently broken off, was not put back together with divine protection," he says. "It was as if I had been reinstated exactly where I had left off, never losing a day."

But of course, much had happened during that six-year gap, and the person flying the fighter was a completely different man. His name was still Kris Mineau, but now he knew God intimately, as a friend. Also, he understood a little better how God's limitless power can be put at the disposal of one weak human being—how God can break through time and space and restore order to those events that have careened hopelessly out of control.

Before long, Kris had an opportunity to demonstrate just how much he does know about the God who guides human events. He was checked out as an F-15 pilot and became a Wings Plan Officer and instructor for this more sophisticated fighter. But in what threatened to be a replay of his previous accident, an engine exploded on takeoff during one of his flights. A fire of magnesium and titanium broke out, and he couldn't put it out with his fire extinguisher.

Although his wing man, the pilot flying in an F-15 beside him, told him to eject, Kris decided to try another approach. With his fear now tempered by a strong faith, he prayed, "Lord Jesus, put this fire out." Immediately, the fire began to die down, and within thirty seconds it went out.

So extraordinary events continue to pervade the life of Lieutenant Colonel Kris Mineau. It's no wonder that he says he frequently feels like shouting from his cockpit, "Eye has not seen, nor ear heard, the things that God has in store for them that love him!"

*　　*　　*

Janice Gravely and Lieutenant Colonel Kris Mineau know as well as any human beings just how totally God can care for those in life-threatening situations. But in a broader view, their terrifying confrontations with death and disaster in the air provide some important lessons for us as we face situations that move out of our control. The threats we face may not be so dramatic. But whatever the challenge, a strong personal faith often emerges as a necessary foundation if miracles are to have the greatest possible impact on our lives.

Of course, God may certainly intervene in a miraculous way in our lives before we become mature believers in Christ. Certainly, Lieutenant Colonel Kris Mineau's first encounter with extraordinary divine power occurred when he really didn't know anything about God. But before he experienced the *full* impact of the miraculous, Kris first established a deep relationship with Him.

Now, let's consider another level of the marvelous world of miracles which almost always seems to lie beyond our ability to control. I'm referring to those elemental energies that have baffled human beings and shaken their confidence since primeval times—the terrifying potential of the unbridled forces of nature.

CHAPTER FIVE

Who Can Harness the Forces of Nature?

We are now about to deal with a subject many people are reluctant to consider. Up to this point, as we've talked about miracles such as healings and rescues from out-of-control airplanes, unbelief could always attempt a rebuttal. The skeptic can always say, "It would have happened anyway," or "That can be explained scientifically"—even if there is no clear-cut explanation.

But try going a little further: Suggest the possibility that mere humans may be able to harness the force of storms, or overcome the power of mighty oceans, or sidestep lethal bolts of lightning. Even in the minds of the faithful, that may seem to be going a little too far. For many, when you venture into these areas, you've crossed the line that separates the extraordinary from the absurd. At best, you risk being charged with advocating superstition, magic, or tricks. And at worst, you're regarded as a charlatan.

Certainly, I don't believe that mere human beings possess the power to control the elements. But I do believe that by proper exercise of gifts God has given us, we can perform greater works than most people dream possible. As we move into this realm of great power, however, it's necessary to recognize certain facts. First of all, the laws of nature were established by God, and not even a cloud moves without His knowledge. His complete control of nature is mentioned frequently throughout the Bible, as in this passage from the Psalms:

"He [God] sends his orders to the world. How swiftly his word flies. He sends the snow in all its lovely whiteness, and scatters the frost upon the ground, and hurls the hail upon the earth. Who can stand before his freezing cold? But then He calls for warmer weather, and the spring winds blow and all the river ice is broken." (Psalm 147:15–19)

God's prerogative to manage the elements also comes across clearly in this series of questions posed by Agur, son of Jakeh, in Proverbs 30:4. "Who has gone up to heaven and come down? Who has gathered up the wind in the hollow of his hands? Who has wrapped up the waters in his cloak? Who has established all the ends of the earth? What is his name, and the name of his son? Tell me if you know!"

The answer to these questions, of course, is "God." Yet there are times, especially in dire emergencies, when humans who have a deep relationship with God can exercise extraordinary power over the land, the seas, and the weather.

In the following pages, we're going to explore how different people have harnessed the forces of nature in extraordinary ways, including:

- miraculous changes in the weather;
- miraculous recoveries from injuries caused by the forces of nature;

• miraculous rescues from natural disasters.

Now, let's take these in order and explore some of the factors that have made each kind of incredible event possible.

Authority over the Elements

You will remember the story of Norvell Hayes who relied on God's power to take command over the weather in his part of Florida and save his orange grove from being ruined by a killer freeze. In that situation, Norvell rebuked Satan. That is, he simply told the devil to take his hands off the orange trees. Then he asked God the Father, in Jesus' name, to surround the fruit trees with His power and not allow them to die. When Norvell took this action, his faith somehow triggered the miracle potential of God's Secret Kingdom. Even though all of the trees on nearby property died, Norvell's trees remained unharmed.

Some observers of this phenomenon, including many of Norvell's neighbors, might argue that the preservation of his grove was just a fluke of nature or a coincidence of some sort. That is, they might say that the miracle was merely an accidental convergence of two unrelated events: 1) Norvell's act of commanding Satan and praying to God, and 2) the immediate salvation of his trees after this prayer.

But Norvell sees things another way. He truly believes that all things are possible with God. On that assumption, he simply took over his plot of ground in God's name and in effect said, "I won't receive this freeze in my grove! God will place a shield of protection over it." And God did just that.

It's true, of course, that God "sends rain on the just and on the unjust," as Jesus said in the Sermon on the Mount. (Matthew 5:45) But that simply means that He loves the entire

101

world—not that he won't grant special benefits to those who have demonstrated their love for Him. In fact, God has innumerable treasures in store for us if we just learn the right way to approach Him in asking for them.

To illustrate this point, I want to describe a personal experience I had with the weather several years ago. Back in the 1960s, Virginia Beach, Virginia, was threatened by a potentially devastating hurricane. This part of the country—which is where the Christian Broadcasting Network offices are located—is in the Tidewater area on the Atlantic Coast.

During the sixties the region had been called "hurricane alley"—and with good reason. Hurricanes would brew in the Caribbean and then sweep up the Florida coast to the Outer Banks of North Carolina. They then crashed through the Hampton Roads area near our headquarters, and finally headed on up the Atlantic Coast. Often, they crossed Long Island, moved up into New England, and then veered out into the North Atlantic, where they diminished completely.

We were afraid that the one predicted back in the sixties would do tremendous damage to our fledgling operation—especially to our broadcasting tower. When we first started the CBN radio and television ministry, we purchased a tower that was about 285 feet high and had a self-supporting base. On top of that, there had been erected another electronic structure some seventy to eighty feet high. And then, above that, was the TV antenna, which rose another thirty-five to forty feet in the air. The total structure was about four hundred feet in height.

We suspected that the TV antenna might be a little too heavy for the support base built for it. In addition, there were none of the guy wires that are usually employed with TV towers. In other words, this gangly, four-legged structure, perching on a relatively narrow base, was virtually devoid of defenses against a big storm. CBN, and all it would become, like a little baby, absolutely defenseless before a hurricane's might. Only someone who has experienced a hurricane knows the awesome destruction they can unleash.

Word reached us that a great killer hurricane with winds exceeding 150 miles per hour was heading directly into our area. We realized further that if the tower was blown over by the high winds, it would fall on our studio—and if the studio was destroyed, that would wipe out CBN. Our resources were so limited then that, short of a miracle, we would have had a hard time recovering from such a disaster.

I immediately knew that our only sure shield of protection was prayer. So I began to talk to God about that hurricane. I described my view of the problem we faced, and I asked for His help. But nothing happened. No answer came to me. Meanwhile, news reports indicated that the hurricane was still bearing down directly upon us.

The next morning, I attended a meeting of the local chapter of a Christian fellowship group—the Full Gospel Business Men's Fellowship. They were holding a Saturday breakfast meeting in the old Monticello Hotel in nearby Norfolk, and more than two hundred people had gathered there that morning. At about 10:30 A.M., I was called upon by the chairman to pray. So I stood up and asked those in the audience to join with me in talking to God about the hurricane.

As I prayed out loud in that meeting, faith rose within me, and with authority in my voice, I found myself speaking to a giant, killer hurricane about one hundred miles away in the Atlantic Ocean.

Specifically, I commanded that storm, in the name of Jesus, to stop its forward movement and to head back where it had come from. By then, it was almost up to Cape Hatteras, North Carolina. Even as I write these words, I know it may seem absurd to talk to a giant hurricane. But that was what the Holy Spirit led me to do, and that's exactly what I did.

After I left the prayer meeting at noon that Saturday, I turned on my car radio. A bulletin on the national news reported that the forward progress of Hurricane Betsy had been stopped at 10:30 A.M. that morning—the precise time when a little group of Christians had ordered it to do so.

According to the meteorologist on the radio, a pressure ridge in one location had encountered a pressure trough in another, and that had halted the forward movement of the storm. The weather people, of course, had a "weather reason" for the unusual change in the hurricane's course. And I don't deny that God may have used natural means to turn those high winds around. But turn them He did. It was almost as though a giant hand had come down out of the sky, blocked that storm, and gestured, "Stop!"

The hurricane stayed where it was for about twenty-four hours. Then, like a great dumb beast obeying its Master's voice, it slowly turned 180 degrees and began to go back down South where it had come from. In the past, we had seen hurricane after hurricane come along the same route, and none of them had ever turned around and headed in the opposite direction. But this hurricane followed orders. God had energized the voice of a man, and a storm had obeyed.

Skeptics may offer other explanations for these events. But I know it was God's power that spared this region and also our CBN tower. As a matter of fact, we haven't had a major hurricane hit Tidewater since then, and that was about twenty years ago. The hurricane activity in our area has apparently been stopped, at least for the present. It's as if God Himself from that time forward has set a kind of shield around us.

I know we have some sort of divine protection because I've seen it in operation when other dangers have appeared on the horizon. For example, we had to face another threat from a major hurricane just two years after the first one. When I heard it was heading our way, I got on the air and asked our viewers to pray along with our CBN employees. On this occasion, we once again rebuked the hurricane in the name of the Lord and commanded it to stay away from our vicinity.

After this, the path this second hurricane took was incredible. It started a landfall at Cape Hatteras, then turned back to sea. Next it went north of our area and immediately turned to land again. Then it turned south, as if seeking entrance to our Hampton Roads cities. But at the border it turned east again, went farther out into the Atlantic, and finally dissipated as if once more an invisible hand—a spiritual force field if you will—had been activated by the voice of a believer to protect our region from harm.

Since that time, not one single hurricane has returned to the region once known as hurricane alley.

Now let's focus on that first hurricane once more because I believe there are some broader lessons to be learned from that experience.

First of all, we were desperate. Our survival was at stake. This was not the polite little prayer of a ladies' church social. We had to have an answer from God or we were ruined.

Stories are told of John Knox who prayed, "Lord, give me Scotland or I perish." Of Moses who prayed, "Spare your people, or blot me out of your book [of eternal salvation]." Of Jesus Christ who was in such an agony of prayer that the capillaries in his face began to ooze blood like sweat. Of John Hyde of India—called "praying Hyde"—who prayed so long and with such intensity that his heart is reported to have shifted in his chest cavity. These men made prayer a life-and-death situation—and they prevailed.

Desperate situations bring about an intensity of prayer that can in turn bring about extraordinary miracles.

Second, God clearly had a stake in the outcome. He had a plan for CBN and for me which did not include being destroyed by a hurricane. Even as I write this chapter, word has reached me that in just one day this week, our West Coast Operation Blessing office in Seattle, Washington, supplied one million nutritious meals to the poor and needy in cities from Los Angeles to Seattle.

In 1962, I could not have known that there would be an Operation Blessing. That came in 1978, sixteen years later. Nor would I have known that in twenty-two years CBN would be playing a significant role in expanding God's kingdom in fifty-six nations of the world. I did not know, but God did. He has a plan for each one of us, and to those who will submit to that plan, He will give the weapons needed to move the mountains of difficulty that stand in the way.

Third, I and most of those present with me were not novices to God's power. For six years, I had studied the Bible. I had saturated my mind with the writings of great men of faith. For two years after receiving Jesus Christ as my Lord and Savior, I had earnestly sought from Him the empowering baptism with the Holy Spirit. And I had received this glorious experience one night in our apartment in Queens, New York, when my oldest son had been instantly and dramatically healed of a dangerously high fever.

For six years, God had permitted struggle, trials, heartaches, yet ever increasing spiritual growth, along with evidence of His miracle power. I knew He performed miracles because the Bible said so—the great saints of history said so—and I personally had seen miracles happen.

Fourth, the group assembled for breakfast on the morning that the miracle took place were there in harmony. There were no sectarian, racial, or sexual rivalries. To the best of my knowledge, there were no personal hurts and jealousies among the people. There was no striving, nor were there hidden agendas for personal advantage. The assembled people loved God and loved one another.

Except for the fact that some of the people were, until that morning, strangers to one another, the scene was somewhat reminiscent of the gathering of the early Christians on the Day of Pentecost. "They were *all together* in *one accord* in one place." Then the mighty power of the Holy Spirit came upon them.

The fact of unity—possibly more than any other single thing—is the key to group prayer for miracles.

Consider these clear statements:

- "If two of you *agree* on earth as touching *anything they shall ask, it shall be done for them* by my Father which is in heaven." (Matthew 18:19)
- "And the Lord said, 'Indeed the people *are one*, and they *all have one language* . . . , now *nothing they propose to do will be impossible for them.*'" (Genesis 11:6)
- "If you abide in me, and my words abide in you, *you will ask what you desire, and it shall be done for you. . . . This is my commandment, that you love one another.*" (John 15:7, 12)
- "I pray . . . *that they all may be one . . .* that the world may believe that you sent me." (John 17:21)

The consequence of unity is awesome. God Himself has said that nothing is impossible for people who have unity and a common purpose. The converse of that is equally true: "A house divided against itself cannot stand."

Christianity is not a solitary religion—whether it be worship or prayer for miracles, it is done better with others. The secret is that each worshiper needs a united heart—no divided allegiance, secret sins, or lack of forgiveness toward others. And then together, those assembled need unity—one accord—on the matter for which they are expecting a miracle.

Fifth, we spoke to the hurricane and commanded it in the name of Jesus to cease its forward motion and to return whence it came.

Perhaps the reason so few people see miracles in their lives is their ignorance of the way power is activated in the universe. God's power underlies all reality. The material world as we see it consists of atoms and subatomic particles, which we further learn are composed of energy in the form of electrons and neutrons. In other words, matter is merely a form of energy. The great paradox is that what we perceive as real and tangible is actually an illusion. The reality is energy; and behind energy is the spiritual power of God.

The order of power in the universe is relatively simple. Beginning with God, spirit controls mind (or thought) and mind controls matter. The conduit for spirit power to the material world is either through the mind or through the voice or through both.

A human being has all three elements—spirit, mind, and body (matter). With many people—especially today—the body and its impulses control the mind and the spirit. Gluttony, alcohol and narcotics, sex, physical achievement, and physical appearance control all else. People controlled by their bodies cannot know God's miracle power.

Others attempt to be controlled by the mind or soul. Some of these people can be very noble, can achieve great successes in business, government, or other worthy professions. Others dabble in soulish or psychic activities. They study mind control, Hindu mysticism, or techniques of gaining riches through mental focus, and others succumb to outright spiritism and satanism.

WHO CAN HARNESS THE FORCES OF NATURE?

Those who attempt to dwell merely on a soulish level may gain dominance and temporary material success, but they will never experience God's power nor will they gain everlasting life.

Those who reach the highest level of power are those who by an act of surrender to Jesus Christ have their spirits re-created (reborn) by action of God's Holy Spirit. They then experience the guidance and direction of their spirits by God's Spirit. In God's perfect order, their own spirits will then control their minds, which in turn will control their bodies. When such people are baptized in the Holy Spirit, their voices become instruments of power to transmit God's benevolent authority over whatever would destroy mankind—be it storm, or disease, or demonic power. This is precisely what Jesus Christ—the perfect man—the God-man—did on earth, and He it was who told His disciples, "The works that I do you shall do and greater works than these because I go to my Father."

Such a person with a renewed spirit and a renewed mind, surrendered to God's purpose, is ready to assume the dominion over this earth that God once gave to the first man, Adam, in the Garden of Eden.

To such a person, what he says is indeed what he gets as this next story illustrates.

My wife, Dede, was caught in a typhoon a few years ago when she was in Taiwan with a group of Christians. They knew that a raging tropical storm was heading in their direction, and if it hit them, there could be great destruction and even death. So they held a prayer meeting to seek God's help. Before the prayer session really got under way, Dede, who was familiar with the correct use of power, went to one of the Spirit-filled leaders and asked him to rebuke the typhoon in the name of the Lord. Quite frankly, he didn't know how to handle such an unusual request, but he sensed she had a point. So as they all prayed, he spoke directly to the typhoon and said, "In the name of Jesus, I rebuke you and command you to go away."

To the amazement of many of these church people, the storm did go away, just as the minister had directed it to do. But it didn't stay away. This particular typhoon was quite persistent and almost seemed to have a mind of its own. The storm went out about a hundred miles into the sea and "decided" that it was going to return. The next morning, when Dede heard it was on the way back toward Taiwan, she went to the man who was leading the group that day and said, "You'd better rebuke that typhoon again."

Unfortunately, this was a different minister from the one who had responded so positively the day before. The new one seemed to be at a complete loss as to what to say or do. It appeared that he wanted to do what Dede asked, but he was confused about how to go about it. So when he prayed, he just said, "Oh God, the storm is coming! Don't let it hurt us!"

Clearly, he had accepted the idea that it was inevitable that the storm was coming, and he saw no point in doing anything to try to stop it. Sure enough, the typhoon moved right in—and in effect, it did as it was "told." The prayer had been, "Don't let it hurt us," and the group wasn't hurt. But the storm swept right over the island, destroyed one billion dollars' worth of property, and left the water unfit to drink for two or three days.

I don't pretend to understand all the dynamics of this sort of incident. In some ways these storms—including the one that Jesus Himself confronted—appear almost to be alive. They resemble a primordial wild beast which only God or God's people can tame. Perhaps there is an element of the demonic in them, a demonic force of evil which can *will* to make the lives of men and women miserable and estranged from God. Or maybe they are just one part of the whole of nature which has fallen along with man. That is, they could be fundamentally good forces which have been estranged from God's ruling hand as a consequence of the loss of man's authority through rebellion against the creator.

Whatever their precise identity, the important point to remember about storms and impending natural disasters is that it's possible for us to exercise God-given dominion over them according to biblical principles.

A Shock from the Skies

The skies around Milwaukee, Wisconsin, were in turmoil on the evening of July 17, 1981. Storms and high winds had been reported in various parts of the state that day, and funnel clouds had been sighted near River Falls and New Lisbon, and just west of Montello. Hail pummeled Eau Claire, Chippewa, and Dunn counties; and a flash-flood warning was posted for still other areas.

It definitely wasn't a good day to be outdoors. But those who must travel or assist travelers don't always have a choice. For Darrell Hines, an airline worker who was also an aspiring gospel singer and composer, the trouble started just after 7:00 P.M. when a thunderstorm began to move through his area. The squall was one of many that were rumbling on the Milwaukee horizon.

As the weather worsened, Darrell, a member of the Republic Airlines ground crew at Mitchell Field, was hard at work assisting a DC-9 from Chicago to land. He guided the plane to its station and then started to lower the plane's stairway. It was at that moment that disaster struck.

Seemingly out of nowhere, a bolt of lightning hit the tail of the DC-9. "From what people tell me, I was going up the stairway when the lightning struck," Darrell says. "It knocked me five feet in the air, they say. But that's just what I've heard. The last thing I really remember was the day before—I can't remember anything on that day."

Two other airline employees were also injured by the bolt. William Rehak had been opening a panel for fuel when the lightning crashed into the plane; he suffered electrical burns to his head and feet, and Gail Breedlove, who was in the process of opening a cargo bag, received electrical burns on her hands and feet.

But both Rehak and Breedlove, who were immediately listed in satisfactory condition at Milwaukee's St. Luke's Hospital, were in much better shape than Darrell Hines: Darrell, in effect, had died after the lightning hit him.

He fell down unconscious after the electricity slammed into him, and two of his co-workers rushed over to his side—but try as they might, they could find no pulse. They immediately started administering cardiopulmonary resuscitation (CPR), but with no result. When the paramedics arrived in their ambulance, Darrell still was not showing any vital signs. His medical records at St. Luke's Hospital, signed by Dr. J. Ebright, describe the situation this way: "The patient fell to the ground. Nearby observers started CPR. Paramedics found the patient . . . without pulse, respiration, or blood pressure."

In fact, Darrell didn't have any pulse or heartbeat for thirty-five to forty-five minutes, says Mrs. Teddy Trimble, a Republic Airlines supervisor who rode in the ambulance to St. Luke's emergency room with him. But although he had barely one foot in this world, the other foot was firmly planted in God's miraculous kingdom—a kingdom in which anything can happen. It was Mrs. Trimble who first noticed the powerful presence of God in this natural disaster. She says that "the Spirit of the Lord" came into the ambulance in a palpable way, and she sensed a miracle might be in the making.

"[The paramedics] continued to work with Darrell to try to revive him," she recalls. "I touched his hand and it was as cold as ice. Then, I said, 'Lord, I just don't believe you're ready to take this young man because I know his ministry and I know his love of you, and I know his love for people. So I just don't believe you're going to take him.'"

As Teddy Trimble continued to pray for him in the ambulance, a reading suddenly appeared on the EKG (the electrocardiogram, which measures heart impulses). "The lines started going up and down, and God brought him back to life," Mrs. Trimble says. "You could feel the power and the presence of God in that ambulance."

Despite these encouraging signs, Darrell was listed in critical condition when he arrived at St. Luke's. A medical team began to work feverishly over him, and their report said he was "groaning, moaning and screaming" in the emergency room. He also moved and jerked his hands and feet about, and shouted, "Oh, Jesus!" according to the official hospital records.

But Darrell's team of helpers wasn't limited to his highly qualified doctors. In addition to Mrs. Trimble's prayers, many other requests for recovery began to go up to God, even in the earliest stages of the injury:

Darrell's mother, who reached the hospital just after the ambulance, began to plead with the Lord immediately after she was notified about the accident. She said, "I didn't know how to pray, but the Spirit began to pray for me. The prayer was, 'Lord, touch Darrell's mind—touch his mind.'"

His wife, Pamela, who was then six months pregnant, was visiting in Memphis when the accident occurred. When her Aunt Elee phoned from Milwaukee with the bad news, the two of them started praying even before they were a minute into the conversation.

The *Milwaukee Sentinel* reported that more than eighty people showed up at the hospital to offer their prayers and personal support. The number of visitors was so unusual that the nurses began to ask, "Who is this Darrell Hines?" Darrell's mother said that they thought he was some sort of rock star.

But despite the broad-based support in those early hours after the lightning struck, things didn't look too good for Darrell. His friends and loved ones heard that he probably wouldn't live through the night. And even if he did live, there was the likelihood of permanent brain damage. Darrell's mother refused to accept such predictions, however. She felt that the Holy Spirit was telling her, "Look past whatever the doctors tell you, and look right at Me!"

That's exactly what she did. She, Darrell's father, who is a minister, and many of their church members continued to offer ongoing prayers for the young man's recovery. Before long, their persistence paid off. His screams and groans finally settled into a repeated supplication: "Bless my soul, Lord." For hours and hours he uttered this short plea. Then he slept.

The next morning he woke up but was suffering from amnesia. He didn't even recognize Pamela.

"When I first talked to him," she says, "he said he had never seen me, said we weren't married. I told him we were going to have a baby, but he wouldn't believe me."

Desperate, Pamela raised up her blouse and showed him her enlarged stomach, but Darrell just said, "That's not my child."

"That really hurt me," Pamela said. "Then he feel asleep after he said that, and I prayed, 'Now, Lord, we asked you for this child, and you've given us this baby.' I couldn't think of the Lord taking him at a time like that. I prayed again, and when he woke up this time, he looked at me and smiled. He said, 'Hi, honey,' and I just praised God for that, for answering my prayer!"

After several additional days of tests, Darrell was released from the hospital as cured. But he was no longer the same Darrell Hines. He had suffered a near-lethal shock of lightning and had lived to tell about it. That would be enough to cause some change in the life of almost anyone. If nothing else, the excitement of such a harrowing encounter with the primeval power of the heavens would imprint a memory that would never fade.

For Darrell, though, the experience involved more than just an exhilarating victory over the frightening forces of nature. That lightning bolt has, in a sense, cast additional light on his very soul. He believes he has been given a second chance at life. As he puts it, he's "more aware of the obligation to share the message of salvation with as many people as possible." He's also more aware than ever before of the miraculous power of the prayers of many faithful believers.

His father has noticed a big change. "He's a new person," Pastor Willie Hines says of his son. "I sometimes used to have to tell him what to do, but now he's completely on his own."

These developments have moved Darrell Hines up to a more exciting spiritual plane. He is a person with a new level of commitment—a commitment based on a personal encounter with the truly limitless power of a God who controls every natural and supernatural event in the universe. Darrell has indeed learned that miracles are still possible, even in the face of one of the most frightening forces of nature.

Mastering a Mighty Ocean

When a person is in the grip of one of the world's great oceans, any attempt to exercise human control may seem foolish. Indeed, unless one has been exposed regularly to the huge, fearsome waves in the middle of a rolling sea, far out of sight of land, it's practically impossible to understand the true power of the deep.

But Warren L. Gallop does understand because he's been there. A former navy man and merchant marine, he knows almost all there is to know about what the sea can do to a ship or a sailor. His seagoing experience has given him as much courage as any single individual can expect when confronted with the elements. Hard-earned wisdom about the waves and weather has provided him with a sure hand on the charter-boat business he runs in civilian life. But for most of his life, Warren, like a modern-day Captain Ahab, tried to wrestle with the stormy seas all by himself. It almost seems that William Ernest Henley, the nineteenth-century poet, might have had Warren in mind when he wrote:

> *I am the master of my fate;*
> *I am the captain of my soul.*

But about ten years ago, Warren finally began to bump up against his own limits as a human being. The realization came in 1972, when he discovered he had throat cancer. His doctors told him he only had a few months to live, and surgery probably wouldn't do much good. Warren was no longer able to control his life, and so he began to look outside himself. He found the answer in a little Methodist Church in Kitty Hawk, North Carolina.

One day, as a hymn was being sung in the church, he heard a voice say to him, "This is your last chance!" At that point, he literally *ran* to the front to make a public commitment to Jesus. A dramatic, spiritual change soon occurred deep inside Warren, and now he *knew* that God was real. He had no doubt about it. In addition, the fear of dying, which had accompanied his cancer condition, left completely.

WHO CAN HARNESS THE FORCES OF NATURE?

One of the first things Warren did after this encounter with Christ was to schedule the surgery that he had been advised wouldn't do any good. He went into the operation knowing that God was in complete control of his life—that God, and not Warren Gallop, was "master of his soul." And the surgery was a success.

Soon the salty, raspy-voiced charter-boat captain, who resembles, as much as any real man can, one of Stevenson's sturdy, seagoing heroes in *Treasure Island*, was back at the helm of his boat. By day, he took fishermen and tourists on trips off the Atlantic Coast. By night, after riding the sometimes intimidating seas, he returned to his warm home in Wanchese, North Carolina, and to his loving wife and prayer companion, Margie.

Although there's usually something of a routine to Warren Gallop's active, outdoor life, the unpredictable seas always hold the promise or threat of something unexpected. And when deep faith is involved also, the unexpected may become the miraculous. The rugged faith that Warren Gallop had been developing for more than a decade—from his conversion through his successful surgery and beyond—was severely tested one day as he was returning from a fishing expedition. The group that had hired his vessel were tired after their outing, and Warren was feeling fatigued himself. He was especially looking forward to spending a comfortable evening with Margie, and so he wasn't too enthusiastic at first when he began to get a contrary message deep inside his being. He sensed someone saying, "Warren, it's not time to go home yet. You have another job to do."

As the internal signals grew stronger, Warren recognized them as special messages that had become familiar during the previous ten years. They were spiritual signals—bulletins from God that indicated something was amiss and His help was needed.

At this urging of the Holy Spirit, Warren changed course and turned west. It seems rather appropriate, by the way, that the name of the Gallop boat is *The Mighty Wind*—a name Warren came across in reading the description of the work of the Holy Spirit in Acts 2:1–2: "When the day of Pentecost had come, they were all together in one place. And suddenly a sound came from heaven like the rush of a mighty wind, and it filled all the house where they were sitting."

As for the other people on the boat, they weren't at all sure what was happening. Imagine the attitude of a tired, hungry weekend fisherman so close to shore that he can almost feel his hot bath and taste his savory dinner, when suddenly the boat he is paying for changes course and heads once again for the open sea. But Warren was decisive, even if indefinite, about the new direction they had taken, and so the passengers limited their grumbling. They had gained sufficient respect for their captain to go along with him without staging an out-and-out mutiny.

But what exactly *was* Captain Gallop about? As the boat churned westward through the rather rough sea, nothing unusual appeared in the water. After they had gone about three and a half miles, Warren himself began to wonder if he really had received a message from God. Or could he possibly have turned aside because of some silly whim of his own?

Finally, in the face of rising resistance on board his boat, he muttered, "This is foolish!"—and he prepared to change course and head back to his own harbor. Then suddenly the answer he had been looking for appeared in the waves ahead.

Two men, hanging desperately on a flimsy raft, lay directly in *The Mighty Wind*'s path. Warren quickly pulled up beside them and hauled them on board—just in the nick of time. Having fought the waves for about five hours after their boat capsized, the young fellows, who were in their mid-twenties, were totally exhausted. Heavy currents had pulled them more than four miles offshore, and they had lost hope of saving themselves. On a couple of occasions they had tried to leave their raft and swim against the current, but they had failed to make any headway. Experienced observers of this part of the ocean felt, in retrospect, that if the hostile waves hadn't gotten them, the sharks in those waters would have.

Warren and the others on board *The Mighty Wind* bundled the two soaked sailors in some warm clothing and helped get their circulation going again. When the boat reached the dock, the men were almost back to normal, and they thanked Warren profusely for rescuing them. He wanted to spend some time finding out more details about their nearly fatal misadventure, but first he had to get his long overdue fishing party disembarked. Unfortunately, when Warren finally turned back to the two waterlogged young men, they had disappeared.

Sometimes our experiences in helping others miraculously—and in being helped—are much like that. Great events like the parting of the Red Sea, Jesus' bringing Lazarus back from the dead, or Jesus' resurrection from the dead, occurred in full public view, with identifiable witnesses and documents to testify to their truth. Even in our own day, a harrowing adventure like that of Darrell Hines in surviving the lethal force of lightning may receive great attention in the press. The event may also generate official records for verification.

But being a part of one of God's miracles doesn't always involve great notoriety or tremendous accolades. Nor are miracles intended to become some sort of "proof" of faith. In many cases, as with Warren Gallop, following God into a miracle may require you to become an "angel unawares," to use the words of the writer of the letter to the Hebrews. In other words, sometimes it must be enough for us just to know, in our most private thoughts, that we've had an extraordinary brush with God's greatest power. In the last analysis, ultimate personal satisfaction and the greatest confirmation of faith must come from within, from that one-to-one relationship we have established with Him.

CHAPTER SIX

Miracles of the Mind

When we think of miracles, we usually remember the most dramatic occurrences. We think of incredible physical healings, or unbelievable rescues from airplanes, or astounding control over the course of violent storms.

But the realm of the miraculous also encompasses those events that are not always so obvious to the eye—though they may be as startling, in their own way, as walking on water. C. S. Lewis says in his book *Miracles* that he uses "the word *Miracle* to mean an interference with Nature by supernatural power." With this definition, he draws in a wide variety of happenings, including startling transformations of the mind.

When we have a brief encounter with another person, that individual's true personality and deepest emotional makeup are usually cloaked in social convention or masked by psychological defenses. But as we get to know the person better, the true state of his or her inner life begins to emerge. In most cases the mentally impaired person is at least partially aware of his problem, including his desperate need for inner healing. Yet physicians and psychologists are often woefully ill-equipped to cure these difficulties. As with the most serious or terminal physical illnesses, the only answer lies outside ordinary medicine, in the realm of faith and the supernatural. It's at this point that the need for a "miracle of the mind" becomes evident.

Now, let's meet several individuals whose inner encounters with God have been at least as dramatic and life changing as any we've yet examined in the outer world.

The Miraculous Mending of a Drug-Damaged Mind

Mike MacIntosh was a high-school dropout—but that wasn't because he lacked ambition. On the contrary, he left school because he was a young man in a hurry, and he certainly didn't plan to let a lack of academic credentials stand in his way.

A native of Poway, California, he possessed a free-wheeling, western-style entrepreneurial spirit that promised to catapult him to super business achievement. Some might say it was his quick, compelling smile that did the trick; others might point to those riveting eyes that could make you feel for a moment as though you were the only person in the world. Whatever the exact reason, by the time he was twenty-two, Mike had learned to apply his considerable skills of persuasion so well that he had attained great success as a car salesman. If you had the remotest need for an automobile when you came into contact with him, you could count on becoming a customer. As a result, he soon had a high income, a comfortable home, three cars, numerous credit cards, and a nice wife—and he was dropping LSD like it was penny candy.

What exactly got this young go-getter off the upward track in business and onto drugs?

122

To begin with, Mike's childhood contributed little to a normal, stable life. His father was an alcoholic and gambler who had deserted Mike's mother when Mike was a small child. His older brother had committed suicide in his teens.

But despite these drawbacks, Mike had a number of things going for him—things that should have made a big difference in his life. All who knew him agreed that he was highly intelligent and a real charmer in human relationships. In fact, this personal magnetism was one of the big factors that helped him marry his wife, Sandy, only two weeks after they had met.

Mike also wanted to find God and do His will, but he seemed to search in all of the wrong places. For one thing, he was a UFO freak who had become obsessed with looking for extraterrestrial beings. He had also tried the occult and various Eastern philosophies and had experimented with psychedelic drugs. In fact, he says, he started taking drugs as part of his effort to find God. But drug addiction soon caused him to lose touch with reality. Things finally degenerated to the point where his wife divorced him.

Mike got deeper and deeper into his drug habit, until finally he hit rock bottom. On one final, fateful occasion, he had been taking acid, or LSD, for about ten straight days, and he was sure he was on the verge of death. His head was spinning with the weird, distorted visions that only a powerful psychedelic drug can produce. Of course, the monstrous shapes existed only in his mind, and the scary perceptions that almost drove him mad were merely overblown versions of ordinary reality. But a drug-damaged mind can't distinguish between what's real and what's not.

Then, Mike says, he had a "revelation" which impressed him with the message that he should never take drugs again. Along with this insight came an intense sense of the love of God. But these sensations of a divine reality were still in the most rudimentary stage, and the shocking state of Mike's mind inhibited any spiritual progress for a time.

In fact, at first it seemed as though the supernatural message might have come too late. As a result of his lengthy bout with LSD, Mike found that something strange and frightening had happened to his mind: He became certain that a huge portion of his head had been blown to bits. Eventually, he was admitted to a mental institution where the prognosis was institutional care for the rest of his life. And he did spend the next ten months in psychotherapy and another seven months in group therapy, where the emphasis was on teaching him to interact with people again.

But social considerations aside, what was going on in Mike's own head during this period is the most disturbing part of his story. He had so abused his mind and body that for two years he literally believed he had been shot in the brain, had lost part of his head, and had died.

It soon became clear that human efforts, such as psychotherapy, weren't going to be adequate to bring Mike back to reality. But another, more potent source of help was at hand. He met some musicians from a church in California who kept inviting him to services: "Hey, man, you'd go for this church scene! Why don't you try it once?"

Finally, he decided to check out the church. He was certainly more cautious about God than he had ever been about LSD. He might have been willing to plunge into a new drug experience, sight unseen, but where Jesus was concerned, he seemed to want to measure his every step before he got involved.

"For a month before I stepped in the doors of that church, I'd drive up and down and look at the cars," Mike says. "During the evening services, I'd sit in the parking lot and watch the hippies come and go. I couldn't believe all those long hairs going to church."

It was as though he wanted to conduct some sort of in-depth demographic survey before he edged a little closer to a commitment—for Mike seemed to realize that the crucial spiritual decision that he was about to face was for keeps.

Finally, he got up the courage to look inside the sanctuary. "When I went in, I felt the same love of Christ I had sensed the night I overdosed," he remembers.

God was making another of those key overtures, and the question was, how far was Mike willing to go in accepting the supernatural offer?

Perhaps the major turning point in his life came when he felt the real presence of God while he was alone one evening. "One night, I thought there was an earthquake," he recalls. "The next day, nobody had heard about it or felt it, and the papers didn't say anything about it. What did happen was a beautiful presence entered my bedroom. I fell out of bed and said, 'God, if I'm having an acid flash or if I'm going to die, take me to heaven!' And a still, small voice said, 'You have been visited by the Spirit of the Lord. If you will follow me, I'll lead you to the people you've always wanted.' I had always wanted to be able to express myself to people, to tell them I loved them and to have them love me. I didn't want to hold anything back."

Finally, Mike had thrown himself heart and soul into Christ's camp—and the level of his commitment continued to accelerate. He soon decided to spend six months living in a Christian commune, and during this period, he studied the Bible and prayed daily. But even with this spiritual progress, there were deep emotional wounds that remained to be healed. Although he felt the presence of God in his life, he still believed he was walking around with half a head, half a brain. The damage inflicted by drugs continued to debilitate him, and he found he couldn't function completely as a thinking being.

He says, "I felt I just had to know—am I alive or dead? I knew I was saved, but did I have a hole in my head? I had [some sort of] brain damage. The whole left side of my brain [seemed not to be] functioning."

Finally, the big miracle of Mike MacIntosh's mind occurred one night at a prayer meeting. "The elders laid hands on me, and I found I was trembling and shaking. My entire head started 'glowing.' [Suddenly], for the first time in two years I had normal feeling."

As he tells it, a great "light" seemed to "explode" in his head, and after that, he was all right. Mike found himself crying and praising God, and he sensed the Lord was telling him that he had been given "the spirit of love and a sound mind."

Nor did Mike's miraculous emotional and mental transformation end with this inner healing. He and Sandy, who also became a Christian, were later remarried, and now they have five healthy, well-adjusted children. In addition, Mike has been serving God in various *mentally* challenging ways since his recovery. After a brief involvement with a music ministry, he began to teach the Bible, which he had been reading and studying five or six hours a day. Later, God led him into a preaching ministry. In other words, Mike quickly became quite effective in using his *entire* brain—the same brain that he and his doctors were sure had been permanently impaired.

Before long, he started a home Bible study class in his apartment with twelve people making up the original group. That small band has since grown into a congregation of more than three thousand people at the nondenominational Calvary Chapel of San Diego. Mike is now the pastor of that church. As part of this ministry, he and his co-workers have founded the San Diego School of Evangelism, with three hundred missionaries who have been sent to twenty different countries. He also

126

conducts evangelistic crusades in Poland, Hungary, East Germany, China, and other countries.

Clearly, Mike MacIntosh's drug-ravaged mind is impaired no longer. Through his growing faith in Christ, the laying on of hands by church elders, and other spiritual power sources, the miraculous healing and energizing power of God has entered his life and overcome the devastation of powerful drugs.

But drugs are sometimes only a part of a more extensive set of emotional problems, as we'll see in our next illustration.

Even a TV Star May Need a Mental Miracle

The *Father Knows Best* television series, which ran and reran on three networks for about nine years, was one of America's most popular situation comedies during the 1950s. There are many factors that go into the making of such a success, but where public performances are involved, you have to have strong, compelling characters to keep an audience loyal for months and even years.

Most TV critics agreed that one of the keys to the success of that show was pert, brown-haired Lauren Chapin, of Irvine, California. She played the part of the younger sister, Kathy. Lauren—also called Kitten by her television parents, Robert Young and Jane Wyatt—was a regular part of the cast for six years.

By any standard, child or adult, Lauren was a super-achiever. For one thing, she was making $1,000 a week when the show ended in 1960, and her work was fun and personally rewarding, as she helped to portray a happy middle-class family with normal middle-class problems. The *Father Knows Best* family members were "good" people who did almost everything good people were supposed to do—and every show ended on an upbeat note, with some moral message conveyed to the viewers. You felt good after watching one of those programs, and I think in the minds of many of the *Father Knows Best* fans, there was a desire to model their own families and personal lives after the warm relationships and well-adjusted psyches portrayed there.

But off camera, things were considerably different for cute, bouncy Lauren Chapin. Her parents had been divorced when she was five. Her mother was an alcoholic. Lauren and her two older brothers were pushed into working in show business when they were quite young—Lauren herself started the working grind when she was only six.

Then, as a fourteen-year-old "has-been" when the series stopped shooting, she found it hard to get acting roles because she had been typecast as an "adorable adolescent." Moreover, she hadn't attended a regular school but had been taught her lessons on the set. This meant that Lauren had been with adult actors most of the time, so she found it hard to adjust to younger people when she finally entered a regular high school.

In short, Lauren had little in common with her peers, developed a feeling of rejection, and began to think of herself as a social misfit. That feeling, coupled with her insecure childhood, led to experimentation with drugs. Experimentation soon gave way to addiction, and this habit, coupled with a general lack of direction, made Lauren's life a living hell during the next fifteen years.

Her lack of success as an adult actress exacerbated her problems. This once-famous TV star found herself working as an airline stewardess, an insurance-claims examiner, a dog groomer, a cocktail waitress, and a carhop.

"You name it, and I did it," she says.

She attempted to escape by getting deeper into pills and drugs. A self-confessed heroin addict, she says she also took up to sixty diet pills a day for a while. Her addiction cost her a one-year jail term on drug charges and nine months in a mental institution.

Lauren's relationships with men were also a constant source of aggravation and failure. She was married three times. The first union ended in divorce. The second was annulled when she discovered that her husband had not received a previous divorce. The third marriage took place in Mexico. Added to these disastrous marriages were affairs that yielded two illegitimate children.

Finally, Lauren's health collapsed when she contracted viral encephalitis, a disease characterized by inflammation and swelling of the brain. Her mind—indeed, her entire life—was in such turmoil that she began to want to destroy herself. By her own admission, she attempted suicide "many, many times" during this stormy period.

"I can remember at the age of maybe fourteen going into my closet, taking a chair, and putting it underneath a coat hanger," she says. "Then I took a scarf, tied it around my neck, and attached it to the coat hanger. Finally, I kicked the chair out from underneath me—but the only problem was, the coat hanger broke."

That was just one of the many flirtations with self-destruction. But even during these terrible trials and emotional and physical pressures, Lauren Chapin still often sensed she had some connection with God. As a child, her mother had sent her to church, and she had enjoyed the spiritual atmosphere. She even sang in the choir, and taught a Sunday School class at one point. But then, she says, she "sort of fell away."

Still, God seemed to be there, even in Lauren's worst personal crises. Even during one of her suicide attempts, she says she kept praying, "Lord, help me . . . help me . . . help me."

But at this point, her sense of the presence of God and her perception of his will were only rudimentary, and were frequently quite distorted. At one of the lowest points of her existence, her roiling emotions combined with a distorted understanding of Scripture to produce a near disaster. She actually tried to cut off her hand after she had been using heroin for seven years. "I was just at the end of my rope. I hated what I'd done to myself. I hated my life. I hated everything."

In this state of depression, she remembered the Bible verse "And if your hand make you sin, cut it off. It is better for you to enter into life maimed, than having two hands, to go to hell, into the fire that shall never be quenched." (Mark 9:43) So in her confused state of mind, she borrowed a meat cleaver from a neighbor, and at 3:00 A.M., she tried to cut off her left hand— the "sinful" hand which she used to shoot dope into her body. Fortunately, the doctors were able to save the hand, but she still lacks feeling in several of her fingers.

Finally, after years of such destructive living, the spiritual seeds that had been planted over time began to bear fruit.

The road to a more stable inner life began in jail, where she was doing time on a drug charge. While there, she met a Dominican priest who told her regularly, "Jesus loves you." She responded by spitting in his face and telling him, "There's no God, and there is nobody that loves me!"

Most people would have given up in dismay at the prospect of working with such a subject. But not this priest. When Lauren left jail and was sent to a mental institution to undergo a drug rehabilitation program, he kept visiting her—even though he had to travel about 150 miles to do so. He came almost every weekend, and, Lauren says in retrospect, "He planted seeds left and right!"

Later, when she was seriously ill in the hospital, another friend came regularly to visit her and pray for her—even though

Lauren told her in no uncertain terms that prayer would do no good. The gentle wooing of God increased in intensity when she left the hospital and went to stay with her brother and sister-in-law, who is a Christian.

"She's the kind that doesn't say much," Lauren says. "But her actions say a whole lot. She left religious pamphlets around when she went to work, and I'd read them. I also read the Bible there, and God just started ministering to my life at that time."

Lauren also began to send her young son to church. But finally he told her, "Mom, I don't want to go to church unless you go with me." This was the last straw. Although she agreed, she laughingly told him that the church would probably crumble when she went in because she was such a sinner.

So Lauren attended services with her son and a neighbor— and this step proved to be the decisive one. "When an altar call was given, I turned around and suddenly realized I was in front of the altar with my hands raised, asking God into my life!" she recalls. "My conversion was a subtle thing, no visions or dramatic supernatural voices. Still, after that public commitment in church, it has been a steady upward climb."

In short, Lauren has now entered into a growing relationship with Christ, and her once-confused mind has been healed. The drugs are gone for good, even though they had been the crutch without which she couldn't function. The suicidal tendencies that regularly tore her apart inside have disappeared. Perhaps most important for her future life, the residual bitterness that made her so unhappy has faded away. "How can you be bitter when God loves you so much?" she says. "I can't be bitter toward anyone."

The miracle in Lauren's life is that a broken, destructive emotional system has been mended, as good as new. Joy and stability have replaced depression and constant turmoil. Of course, she acknowledges that the Christian life is not easy, and she continually faces new hurdles that God must help her surmount in her movement toward a closer relationship with Him.

But gradually, things have been falling into place. Now she has a job she likes very much, and she is living happily in a strong Christian environment with her two children. As a matter of fact, she's just across the street from her brother and sister-in-law, those strong Christians who nudged her onto the right spiritual path years ago.

Where strain and pain once cast a shadow over her countenance, her face now is more likely to shine with an exuberant smile. Where inner turmoil once upset her entire life, a supernatural peace and tranquillity now reign. In short, Lauren Chapin has discovered the secret of bringing miracles into her ravaged emotional life. Her special miracle was as profound as the stilling of a hurricane at sea.

A Rapist Forgiven

Deep inside every creature is the instinct for self-preservation. Yet in some animals and in many people, the instinct to protect their young or their mates is even more intense. Awesome, dangerous rage can rise up in a bear whose cubs are threatened or a stallion in defense of his mares.

So it is with human beings. An otherwise gentle man will go insane with rage toward someone who injures or sexually molests his wife. Gracious, loving women have been known to turn into scheming, venomous shrews in defense of their children. In fact, one diminutive mother marshaled the incredible strength needed to lift an automobile that was crushing her son to death.

I can illustrate this phenomenon most clearly by asking each male reader to close his eyes and visualize his wife tied half naked on a bed, being sexually molested by a fifty-year-old, sallow-faced, sexual deviate. What would your reaction be toward the rapist as you heard the woman you loved screaming and begging for help?

Some men would kill. Others would beat the attacker into insensibility. Others would want retribution from the law. "That dirty _____ should never walk the streets again." In a case like this, forgiveness of the rapist and cleansing of the memories would constitute a divine miracle.

Consider now the case of Larry Benton. Larry was a big, burly ex-marine who looked as if he could quickly overpower anyone who crossed him. He adored and respected his wife, Beverly, intensely. His dominant presence, and the circumstances of their life as Campus Crusade for Christ workers, had never made it necessary for him to worry about defending her physically before.

But that all changed in a dramatic stroke one fateful day. As Larry was working at his desk in Southern California, he received a frantic telephone call from his next-door neighbor. It took a few moments for the ominous nature of the message to sink in: "A man has broken into your house and hurt your wife!" Larry's friend cried. "I think he took her car. Can you come right home?"

As Larry rushed home, he didn't know exactly what he would find, but he feared the worst. Trapped in an emotional maelstrom, he found himself asking, "Why, why, why did this happen?" Yet even as he cried out, he knew instinctively there was only one source from which he could get a meaningful answer—and so he began to pray.

During that drive, he maintained a steady stream of communication with God: "Dear God, I know you're in charge of everything, and you either cause or allow all that enters our lives. . . . I know you didn't cause this, but you did *allow* it! Why? . . . You've promised to make all things work together for good, but how can you do it in a case like this? . . . I know you've commanded us to give thanks in everything, and although I don't feel like it, I thank you by faith. . . . Please, God, use this to your glory!"

When he reached his house, Larry saw at a glance that the family car was gone. The front door was open, and when he looked inside, he noticed that several of his belts were in the hallway, knotted together. On the verge of complete panic, he ran to his neighbor's house, where he found Beverly in her bathrobe. Her face was bruised, and she was crying convulsively.

From what he could piece together from Beverly in her distraught condition, a stranger had forced his way into the Benton home and sexually attacked her. At first, Beverly had struggled with her assailant, but soon she realized she was powerless to defend herself. Eventually, the man tied her up with some of her husband's belts—and then he had the gall to use Larry's razor to shave. He also changed into some of Larry's clothes before leaving.

But even in the midst of the violence and abuse, the miracles began. Although Beverly had been physically and emotionally hurt and shaken, she somehow managed to summon the inner strength and presence of mind to begin to talk with the rapist about Jesus Christ. Can you imagine? Here was a woman who had suffered a supreme degradation. At the very least, she must have felt numb and been heading toward a total lack of control. Hysteria, unfeeling shock, or murderous anger would have been her most logical emotions.

Yet something beyond mere logic was happening here; something truly miraculous was taking place. Instead of withdrawing or lashing out, Beverly *reached* out—to the one who was her greatest enemy at that moment. But the man rebuffed her. He said that he was going to keep on committing one crime after another "because the world is in such a mess." In any case, he certainly wasn't interested in God.

But Beverly kept after him—again, with that superhuman love. She told him that breaking the law wasn't the answer. "Christ in the hearts of men is the answer to peace in this world," she said.

None of this seemed to touch the man—at least not in any profound way. But if you listened closely to him, something seemed to be happening on some level. Before he left, he told her, "I had planned to kill you, but you can thank your God that I didn't." And then he disappeared, taking her car to make a getaway.

Then the special power from God left Beverly, and the full physical and emotional impact of her incident hit her. After she reached their neighbor's house, she couldn't control her emotions any longer. For that matter, neither could Larry. When he charged in and heard his wife tell her story, his rage knew no bounds. The ex-marine, now fully aroused, said, "If I had come home while this was going on, I'm sure I would have killed the man!"

Soon the police arrived to conduct an investigation, and Beverly was rushed off to the hospital. Still, even though safety had returned to his home—and at least everyone was alive— Larry didn't experience any immediate relief from his burning hostility. Instead, tremendous bitterness and anger welled up inside him that night after the attack—so strongly that it would have been easy for him to cast aside all restraint and go out to stalk the offender. Revenge is one of the most powerful drives we have, especially if we're injured at a sensitive point. And

Larry, through his wife's suffering, had been wounded and threatened in the deepest recesses of his being.

But in the course of time the attacker was caught. Soon he was convicted and sent to prison, and the Bentons' car was returned. The memory of the assault still lingered, however. It remained a source of unease in the life and relationship of Larry and Beverly. The mere thought of the intruder had the power to frighten Beverly in nightmarelike flashes through her waking and sleeping hours, and to make Larry violently angry.

So Beverly and Larry were ordinary human beings, with ordinary human emotions. But they also were Christians who knew that the inner turmoil they were feeling wasn't what God wanted for them. By themselves, they seemed unable to change the way they felt. When Larry looked at the assailant objectively, he knew there was reason to feel sorry for the man because of his wasted life. The attacker had a long criminal record; in fact, he had been in trouble since the age of twelve. He certainly had no reason to be happy and satisfied, as the Bentons had been before the attack occurred.

But these were just rational arguments, without the power to change the deepest-rooted attitudes and emotions. Larry still couldn't bring himself to feel sorry for the rapist. When you've been violated, physically and emotionally, it's practically impossible to alter the way you feel—at least it's impossible if you're trying to accomplish this on your own. With God, though, nothing is impossible. And Larry and Beverly believed in God. They had always been convinced He could do anything. Now, the crucial test had arrived. Could He transform and heal their wounded minds and emotions? Could He eradicate the deep scars, the hatred, the bitterness, and the fear?

First of all, they simply asked God to "redeem" the situation, or to use it for His purposes in some way. You'll recall that just after the incident occurred, Larry had prayed, "Although I don't feel like it, I thank you by faith. Please, God, use this to your glory."

To many, it may seem ludicrous to thank God after your wife has been sexually attacked. After all, what's there to be thankful about? Yet Larry knew that the Bible, which he accepts as the ultimate authority in these matters, says we should thank God in all circumstances. (I Thessalonians 5:18) So against all his natural logic and those strong, hostile feelings, he did just that.

As for Beverly, she almost immediately assumed a thankful attitude, even though she had been the target of the violence. As she and Larry went into the emergency room at the hospital just after the attack, she told him, "Honey, when you think you have only a few minutes to live, there are a lot of things that aren't important. You think in your heart, 'Already, God is beginning to work this together for good.'"

So even though they had no idea how it would happen, the Bentons continued to expect God to turn their terrible situation around, to transform it from evil into good. In an effort to move even closer to God during this crisis, they also *forgave* the assailant. As we've seen before, communication with God will be blocked and miracles may become impossible if we approach our problems with an unforgiving heart. As difficult as it may be, it's necessary to give up the hatred or bad feelings we have toward others if we want God to do big things in our lives.

So during these emotionally tough times, Larry and Beverly came to a "new understanding of why [God] wants you to forgive others, even as He, for Christ's sake, has forgiven you." As a firm anchor to ensure his commitment to this principle, Larry took hold of Ephesians 4:32 as his biblical authority—a passage that urges Christlike forgiveness.

But if you think being obedient to God's commands to love and forgive was hard for Larry and Beverly up to this point, tougher challenges were yet to come. The couple began to sense that God wanted them to tell the assailant about their faith in Him. As the magnitude of such a task begins to sink in, the prospect of going through with it may seem completely impossible. After all, how can any husband or wife bear the thought of contacting such an attacker again and then actually take steps to help him? But as we've seen, with God all things are possible.

So they sat down and wrote to the man, who was now an inmate in prison, and told him that through the love of Christ, they had forgiven him. They also described how he, too, could receive the power of God into his life. The prisoner, whose name was Carl, soon wrote back and indicated that he was open to hearing more about this God who appeared to be doing such dramatic things in the Bentons' lives.

Of course, it's easy to be cynical about such an encounter. Some might suspect that the convict had ulterior motives in encouraging this kind of contact. But the Bentons weren't naïve. They were completely aware that the man might have some angle he was working on to benefit himself. It's just that they were willing to take the chance.

So they pushed for a closer relationship with the convict. As an initial step, they arranged to visit him at Folsom Prison, where they planned to share their faith with him in person. Though nervous at first about the meeting, the Bentons soon warmed up to the man and actually began to enjoy the conversation.

"You have no idea what this means to me," Carl said, as he revealed that they were the first people who had visited him.

The Bentons continued to keep in touch, and about three years later, they heard that Carl had asked Christ to come into his life. This may seem to be the high point in our story, or perhaps even the final chapter. But often, it's easy to let important, dramatic spiritual commitments like this fade into the past, without further building and nurturing. There's a tendency to let relationships slip. We may share the Gospel with a stranger, or perhaps treat a poor person to a meal, but that's the end of it. Assuming that our duty is done, we fail to follow up. But that wasn't the Bentons' way.

When Carl came up for parole, they went to bat for him and offered to help him find a job and a place to live in the community. Larry even went before the parole board and testified to the officials that it was Christ's love that had prompted him to help Carl.

The parole board members had never before had the husband of a sexual assault victim plead for mercy for the criminal. In fact, it was an unheard-of turn of events anywhere. As far as they were concerned it was "beyond reason." So understandably, the parole board was impressed. Largely as a result of the support the Bentons showed for Carl, the board released him into their care on parole some four years and eight months after he entered prison. The circle was now complete. The hostility the Bentons had once felt was gone. In its place was an incredible love. The man who had wronged and debased them so thoroughly had now returned—but as their team member instead of their terrorist.

"I've changed," Carl said. "My attitudes have changed; my life has changed. I don't want to do the same things I've done. I don't want to steal anymore. I want to serve the Lord, and I'm happy doing that."

Carl was given training by the Campus Crusade staff, and he made a good start on his new life of faith. But his experience hasn't been without its ups and downs. At one point, he had to go back to prison for several months because he left the state without authorization. But the Bentons, always steady and forgiving in their love, kept up their friendship. Now Carl is working with them in a prison ministry.

So clearly, the final result has been nothing short of a miracle of changed feelings. Against all "normal" human inclinations, God cleansed the hate and bitterness from all three people and thus freed them to help others with similar problems.

In describing their growing prison ministry, Beverly says she "felt a compassion" to understand what would drive people to commit terrible crimes. "So I started to work with women in jail. I was then led to work with them in prison. I believe if we had not been willing to forgive Carl, we would not have been blessed the way we have been. As a result, we have seen hundreds of people come to know Christ."

Hatred and a desire for revenge may be the most natural feelings in the victim and in her loved ones after a sex offense. But they are also extremely destructive emotions that can deepen inner scars and make the injured person shrivel and die inside. The prospects are considerably different for those with the necessary courage—and the reservoirs of mature faith—to probe the miracle dimension, even in the midst of violence and abuse. For these adventurous souls, doors may well open to supernatural transformations of the mind—and to even greater personal growth than would have been possible without the tragedy.

The Miracle of Freedom from Paralyzing Fear

Fear of any sort can cripple the mind and emotions. But when it gets as serious as it did with Linda Tyrrell, life may seem to be finished.

The outward appearance of this jolly-looking young New Jersey brunette belied the turbulent emotions just beneath the surface. She suffered from a fear known as agoraphobia—a term literally meaning "fear of the marketplace," now used to describe various irrational fears of being in open spaces, or in public places where people congregate. Like any other kind of neurotic fear, such as claustrophobia, there are degrees of agoraphobia. But with Linda, things gradually grew worse. She eventually became virtually a prisoner in her own home—simply because of her morbid fear of going outside.

The condition appeared first just after she experienced the trauma of going through a divorce, and it got progressively more serious during the next four and a half years. "I would go into a panic when I went out alone," she says. "I would get shaky all over, and my heart would pound like crazy. My legs felt like wet noodles—as though they were going to collapse any minute."

It was also hard for her to breathe, she says—a classic physiological sign that fear and anxiety had taken control. But the worst part was that she actually wanted to scream for help whenever she went out alone. In fact, she *did* start "screaming inside her head"—and sometimes she felt she might go insane.

Finally, Linda reached an emotional rock bottom: "I didn't even like to think about going out. The fear just grew worse and worse and worse."

This emotional paralysis led to a deep sense of frustration and depression. Linda also realized she had "a lot of anger, hostility, resentment, and bitterness" in her heart. But she seemed unable to do anything about these feelings.

"I hated the world and myself," she says.

In an effort to relieve the almost unbearable inner pain and misery, Linda started taking tranquilizers and antidepressants. She also drank a lot and smoked two packs of cigarettes a day. Other parts of her attempted rehabilitation program included sessions with a psychiatrist and two psychologists, and also group therapy. But none of these measures did much to solve her problems.

Linda's father tried to help her, but she didn't respond positively to him or any other family members. In fact, she took out her frustrations by yelling at her daughter; and the agoraphobia continued to get worse.

The word *miracle* hadn't been a part of Linda's life up to this point. But she knew she needed something extraordinary if she hoped to live a normal life. So, as a last resort, she turned to God.

But Linda's personal probes into the spiritual dimension were rather tentative at first, taking several different approaches. Christianity was one of the front-runners at first. At one point while she was watching a religious broadcast, she even asked Jesus to take over her life. The pressures did ease up on her a bit after that. But she didn't follow up on her decision. The only way I know to grow after making an initial commitment is to develop a regular, in-depth prayer life; to establish close relationships with other believers, and to get involved in a systematic study of the Bible.

But Linda didn't rely on these essential sources of spiritual growth. Instead, she drifted back into her old, fearful patterns and even got sidetracked into the occult. Anyone in the early stages of any spiritual experience is open to a variety of supernatural influences, some good and some quite dangerous. Unless you pay close attention to the major sources of inner development that Jesus and His Apostles established, anything can happen. You may remain in the same spiritual spot, making no progress whatsoever. Or you may even start moving backward, farther and farther from God's presence.

So Linda ended up quite confused. She seemed unable to find the right door that would open into a fuller life. Then one day, she found herself watching our *700 Club* television program—and the timing was just right. It's not that there aren't other presentations of the Gospel available, because there are. But any word from God will fail to change a person's life unless that person is ready to receive. This time, the word and the listener were on the same channel. Linda, upon hearing the Good News of Christ, decided to reach out and call our counseling center. After pouring out her heart to one of the counselors, they prayed together, and Linda was ushered directly into the realm of miracles that can transform the emotions.

Specifically, Linda and the counselor agreed on the phone that God could and would heal her mind. Then she really began to *expect* something to happen. The result was that their faith and the counselor's prayer activated the miracle-working power of God which was needed to eliminate Linda's paralyzing fears.

"After the counselor prayed, I started to feel tingly," Linda recalled. "It started in my legs and went through my whole body. I felt beautiful. And then she said, 'Honey, you are healed!' I was so happy and excited I couldn't contain myself. I threw away my cigarettes, depression, pills, resentment, anger, hate, guilt—and the agoraphobia. I was and still am free! Jesus Christ touched me and made me whole. He gave me a brand-new life."

Overcome with joy and excitement, she ran out of her house—without any fear—and went to see her father to tell him what had happened. Also, as a kind of spiritual bonus, she hugged her father for the first time with real love. "Before I was healed, I couldn't or didn't know how to love him," she says. "But Jesus put a love inside my heart that wasn't there before."

Linda's feelings instantly and miraculously changed from all-consuming fear and hate to God-inspired love. She says Jesus has also given her "a peace that goes beyond understanding."

143

This mental healing has also brought about a complete change in her activities. Now, instead of clinging to isolation in her home, she is constantly on the go, mixing with others and helping them anyplace, anytime. Her field of operations ranges from nursing homes to her church to various fellowship groups. She actually looks forward to meeting others and helping them. The paralysis of fear has no place in Linda's life, and the jolly, buoyant look that comes so naturally to her is no longer skin-deep. These days, Linda Tyrrell is a joyous, confident person through and through.

The Supernatural Softening of a Crime-Hardened Heart

What happened to Arthur Meunier, beginning in the days of his early childhood, smacks of scenes from some unbelievable horror story. When he was only three, his parents, who were Canadians, died in a boating accident. He was adopted by a couple who actually *taught* him thievery and hatred. His adoptive mother made him steal groceries, and his adoptive father urged him to steal coal from the railroad. Arthur didn't question this home training. He just assumed that what the adults told him to do was right and proper, and he did it.

By age eleven, Arthur was a confirmed thief, but he certainly didn't enjoy the way of life that had been forced on him. He hated his adoptive parents, and they didn't like him too well either. The woman beat him until his ribs, nose, and jaw were broken. Then, in the winter of 1936, they threw him, bleeding, out of the house into the snow.

Unfortunately, the local government authorities couldn't find a foster home for young Arthur. So they put him in the county jail for two years. This became another in the unending series of bad breaks that had plagued the boy. Some of his cell-mates tried to attack him; others tried to guard him from harm as best they could. But there was no way that occasionally present, well-meaning prison inmates could preserve a youngster from physical and emotional abuse in that sort of environment. Things got so bad that he was once given twenty-one strokes on the bare buttocks, and he lost consciousness during the beating.

Predictably, when Arthur was released from jail at age thirteen, he was terrified and lonely. Despite the terrible things that had happened to him there, jail was the only home he knew; so he soon decided to return to his familiar, if far from perfect berth behind bars. To this end, he stole a piece of lead pipe from a plumbing shop and then turned himself in to the Canadian police.

Two years later, Arthur was released again, and this time decided on a change of scene. He emigrated to the United States, but the new locale didn't mean he was about to turn over a new leaf. Instead, he continued to pursue a life of crime—though certainly not as some elusive, master criminal. He had so much trouble evading the law that during the next forty-two years, he spent only about eight or nine weeks out of prison. Twenty-four of these years were spent in solitary confinement, and at one point he was chained by the neck to the wall of his cell for thirty-one months. The only life Arthur Meunier knew was a life behind bars.

"You name it, I did it," he says, reflecting on his crime-ridden life.

"I was demon-possessed with hate," he says. "The word *God* nauseated me." And it was this hatred that kept him going during the years of solitary confinement.

Some might say such a deeply ingrained pattern of outlaw living is impossible to change, and perhaps it *is* impossible as far as natural solutions are concerned. The hardened criminal, the repeat offender who appears impervious to reform, is usually written off in our society. Certainly, judges and juries tend to load him with guilty verdicts and heavy sentences. Rehabilitation for such a person is "beyond reason."

But a belief in miracles presupposes that the supernatural can soften the heart of even the hardest criminal. But what about a man like Arthur Meunier?

The possibility of the miraculous first entered Arthur's life when a Christian family came to the federal penitentiary at Leavenworth, Kansas. They were scheduled to lead a service in the prison chapel, as they did regularly on a volunteer basis. At the time, Arthur was confined in a cell just across from the chapel, and he couldn't help hearing the singing. Somehow, the music touched him. For the first time since his adoptive mother had beaten him and thrown him out of her house, he cried.

Later that day, the parents from the family of singers tried to talk to him, but he rebuffed them. But then their fourteen-year-old son glanced at Arthur through the bars of his cell and winked. Somehow, Arthur felt as if the boy were saying, "You're a big phony! You're not as bad as you think you are—and God's going to take care of you!"

Curious, Arthur asked the teenager to return to talk with him. At first he was abusive toward the boy. But the youngster had a kind of divine self-confidence—and he also had a sense of humor. The boy just responded, "I love you," and that threw the convict completely off balance. Arthur knew how to deal with hostility, but not with compassion.

Somehow, the inmate knew that he was in touch with some force that could be extremely important to his future. But he was still confused. What was this boy trying to prove? Arthur wondered. Was he really on the level, and if so, did he truly know what he was talking about? To resolve some of these questions, Arthur entered into a correspondence with the boy.

"Every letter he sent me was a testimony or a sermon," Arthur says.

Finally, in 1970, about seven months after that first meeting, Arthur committed his life to Christ. Gradually, as the power of God worked in his life, Arthur changed. He continued to correspond with the youngster and to receive visits from him for a total of seven years. And during this period, the inmate began to taste an eternal dimension of reality that he had been completely unaware of before.

But then tragedy struck. That boy, whom God had used to lead a hardened criminal to Christ and to help his new faith grow, was killed in a traffic accident while he was en route to visit Arthur in jail.

Arthur Meunier was a different person now, however. The death of his young spiritual mentor only seemed to spur him on to faster spiritual development. Then, in an action that was totally out of character for the tough guy he had been in the past, he asked forgiveness from the prison authorities for the way he had treated them. And after further prayer, he felt he had to make restitution to those he had stolen from. So he actually wrote to various police departments asking for names and addresses of his victims. Finally, with the money he had earned in prison at twenty-eight cents an hour, he paid back everyone he could. Something had definitely happened to this career criminal, who had been so ready to break the law.

By 1975, the change in Arthur's life had become so apparent that he was transferred to a minimum-security prison. And although he was illiterate when he first went to jail as a boy—and cared nothing for improving his mind—after his conversion, he obtained a B.A. degree in psychology and sociology by correspondence.

Finally, in 1977, Arthur was released from prison. Adjusting to the outside was terrifying, he says, but God gave him strength and courage in miraculous proportions. He had never eaten a banana split, never been on a subway, and never even seen the new-model cars. He was also unsure about how to pursue honest work. But once again, God showed him the way. Now, he is "self-employed for the Lord," he says. As an ordained minister, he conducts a youth evangelism program; he also works with prisoners and is a prison consultant. Prison officials often ask him to negotiate with inmates for them.

In describing the magnitude of the miracle of a changed heart and mind, which began with a young boy's wink, Arthur says: "Years ago, when things went wrong, I'd injure or kill someone at the drop of a feather. Today, I thank God I can accept each day trusting His divine will. This is simply because hate can be terminated, and love—the real genuine kind of love I know—is eternal."

A Dramatic Blessing for a Hopelessly Handicapped Child

The story of young Les Lemke has thrilled thousands of viewers on such shows as *The 700 Club, That's Incredible,* and *The CBS Evening News with Walter Cronkite.* The account is also familiar to readers of major publications like *The Reader's Digest.* But I have a special interest in taking a second look at this incident because the Lemkes made such a deep impression on me when they visited our center in Virginia Beach, and I'm continually impressed by the amazing miracle God has worked in their lives.

The story begins when a little boy, Leslie, was abandoned by his real parents at Milwaukee Hospital. The doctors found that he had severe mental retardation because of cerebral palsy, and his eyes had to be surgically removed as a result of disease.

He was totally helpless—and totally unwanted. The only people who would take him in were May Lemke, a nurse-governess, and her husband, Joe.

While some people would have given up completely on helping Les develop any physical or mental abilities, May accepted the challenge as "a job to do for Jesus." She devoted her entire attention to him and began praying with a power that is seldom seen. She showered him with love and actually treated him just like a normal child—even though he was anything but normal in those early days.

At first, he couldn't eat, move, or even suck on a bottle. She tried to force the bottle into his mouth, but he still couldn't get the milk out. So she taught him the proper action by making loud sucking noises against his cheek.

As he got older, it was evident that he was incapable of standing or even of moving. But May wasn't one to give up. She strapped Les to a leather belt and dragged him around to train him in moving his body. After three long years of this sort of activity, he finally managed to totter onto his feet and even to walk a little by holding on to a fence and following it with his hands. But progress seemed hopelessly slow to everyone—except to May and Joe.

Though May had been praying all along, she began a new prayer for Leslie when he was twelve. Several times a day, she prayed, "Dear Lord, the Bible says that you gave each of us a talent. Please help me find the talent in this boy, who lies there most of the day and does nothing."

Soon after that, when he still couldn't walk by himself or talk, May and Joe put a piano in his room as a kind of symbol of what they ultimately wanted for him. To others, this gesture may have seemed like a silly waste of money, and the instrument sat there unused. In the meantime, May played all kinds of music for Les on the radio.

One night when he was eighteen years old, May prayed especially hard before putting Leslie to bed. When she left his room, he was sleeping peacefully, lying there as he usually did, unable to talk, or even get out of bed for that matter.

Then something inexplicable happened.

At about three that morning, May and Joe woke up hearing Tchaikovsky's Piano Concerto No. 1, popularly known as "Tonight We Love," echoing in their ears.

"The boy's got music coming out of his room," May told her husband. "Did you leave the television set on?"

"No," Joe replied, somewhat bewildered.

So May went downstairs to investigate. And what she came upon was, indeed, a miracle. Leslie, who had never talked or moved by himself in his life up to that point, had dragged himself to the piano and was playing *and* singing the famous melody, from start to finish. Beautifully!

May started laughing and crying at the same time. "Oh, thank you, dear Jesus, thank you!" she exclaimed. "You have given the boy a talent. Nobody can ever tell me there is no God and Jesus in this world!"

Psychologists and neurologists who have examined Leslie have no real explanation for this phenomenon. They think that the part of his brain that controls musical ability may have been stimulated by music and sound, and then raced ahead in its development. But in the last analysis, what's happened is beyond reason and the ability of science to explain. He has been labeled by doctors and scientists as an "idiot savant," or "wise idiot," because he needs to hear a song only once on radio or television and it's forever recorded in his mind, whether the words are in English, French, Italian, or some other language.

But even if the experts don't know quite what to make of Leslie's transformation, May certainly does. This little woman, who has since taught him how to walk, talk, eat, and show his emotions, has no doubt that it is God who has enabled Les to play the piano without ever having had a lesson.

What can we learn about miracles from May's experience?

To answer this question, let's think back on some of the faith steps she took before this dramatic miracle occurred in her life:

Faith Step 1: May loved Les unconditionally. The boy may have seemed unlovable to others because of his handicap, but May saw only a child desperately in need of help. When she invested her love in him, "All the love in the world came into my house," May says. "After all, what did God, what did Jesus say to everybody? 'Love one another as I have loved you.'"

Faith Step 2: She prayed specifically. May prayed several times a day and every night, and she was very specific about her requests: She asked God to give Leslie a talent. As she puts it, "I believed so much in God or Jesus, I just knew I was going to get something."

Faith Step 3: She persevered. Although it's possible to convey the gist of this story in a few pages, the changes in Leslie didn't unfold in a matter of just hours or days. No, it took eighteen whole years before the great miracle occurred, when Les demonstrated his incredible talent. In a powerful testimony to the importance of patience, May advises, "If you don't get an answer right away, it doesn't mean that you're not going to be answered one way or another. So you've just got to keep right at it, and it will come sometime."

Faith Step 4: She put her money where her faith was. In a sense, May put her faith on the line when she bought that piano before Leslie could even walk. It cost $250, along with the little bench that was placed there in readiness for the boy. Without the availability of that physical prop, Leslie would have had no instrument on which his great, miraculous gift could have been expressed.

The miracle of Les Lemke's transformed mind is perhaps the best note on which to end our discussion of how God can intervene supernaturally in our inner lives. Many times, it's hard to see dramatic changes at first because by definition mental and emotional miracles take place inside us. But in Les's case, the inner miracle immediately became outwardly apparent in his ability to play beautiful music. He now plays regularly before church and secular audiences, both on the stage and as part of television programs. So with Les, the circle connecting a private reality with a public testimony to the power of God has been completed. His experience should remind us that even though some supernatural events may not be so obvious at first, that doesn't mean they are any less real or important.

Now let's turn to a kind of miracle that tends in almost every case to be much more visible. In fact, this topic is sometimes so obvious that it becomes ostentatious, and it may even cause some people to become doubtful that God can be operative through it. I'm referring to the sometimes creative, sometimes crass, but absolutely necessary realm of getting and spending money.

CHAPTER SEVEN

God's Marvelous System of Money Management

Now we're going to spend a little time on miracles involving money—how to get more wealth if you really need it, and also, more important, how to manage your money and use it in line with God's overall plan for your life.

Two of the "laws" of God's invisible Kingdom relating to finances, which I mentioned in my previous book, *The Secret Kingdom*, are the Law of Reciprocity and the Law of Use. I won't try to describe those in detail here, except just to say this.

- The Law of Reciprocity is based on Jesus' statement "Give and it will be given to you. . . ." (Luke 6:38) In other words, even though we should not be motivated to give in order to get something, we can still expect blessings to flow in when our generosity flows out.
- The Law of Use is founded on the biblical principle

that we must take what the Lord has given us—our talents and abilities, as well as material goods—and put them to work for His purposes. Moreover, we should do a good job of managing and improving upon the things we already have.

But there is much more to the miraculous ways that God can take "mammon"—or material possessions that tend to debase us and distort our values—and transform it into monetary blessings that can build us and others up. Here are a few spiritual case studies to illustrate what I mean.

A Miracle Big Enough for Texas

Rhine County is nestled deep in the heart of Texas. It's called the "land of milk and honey" because it produces more of these products than any other county in the state.

The county also has oil. But the chances of finding enough to make any money in an area where there hasn't been a strike are one out of fifty. Yet a while back, against all the odds, investor Don Dalbosco struck black gold in Rhine County. His drillers brought in gushers in a number of new places, and they succeeded much more often than anyone else seemed able to do.

How exactly did Don do it?

Frankly, his methods for locating oil are somewhat unconventional. He says he gets his drilling information from God. "So far, the Lord has shown me where oil and gas are by visions and by the word of knowledge," Don explains.

For example, he says God might "show" him in his mind's eye a map of the state of Texas. Then, the divine hand will point out one particular area, as if a marker were being put down there.

"It's like looking at a movie, a very intense-colored movie," Don says.

When Don gets one of these messages, he follows the instructions without any question. First he thanks God for letting him know the location, then he checks the place out, and finally, he proceeds as though he fully expects to find oil there. And his record for strikes is phenomenal.

As Don's oil business expanded, his competitors became frustrated and jealous of his uncanny ability to ferret out oil pockets when they couldn't. But before long, Don discovered that things had gone far beyond mere jealousy. For one thing, he found his office was being bugged. Moreover, he was hit with six lawsuits, which involved a five-year court battle and the tying up of thousands of dollars of his money, which he would have preferred to be using for oil exploration.

In one incredible case, another company blatantly ignored Don's drilling rights. He warned them they were violating leases by drilling in the wrong location. But the company continued to drill and struck oil. Then, in a move that would throw almost anyone off guard, they claimed the well was dry. To add insult to injury, they filed a lawsuit against Don's company.

Despite all this pressure, Don never gave up. He believed the Lord wanted him to be successful in the oil business. As he told us, "I learned patience, and I also learned that 'no weapon formed against you shall prosper.' The Lord always comes to your aid when you're in need. He will always come to you and help you."

I learned about Don's experiences because our 700 Club counseling center in Houston, Texas, frequently received telephone calls from him asking for prayer. Our area director there also remembers that God unraveled each legal complication Don faced.

"It was amazing how God answered Don's prayers and unwound all of the court cases and problems," the director says.

In fact, to the surprise of all his competitors, Don came out on top in every lawsuit. As a result of these victories, he was free to drill in some locations that had been forbidden to him during the legal battles. But there was still a big problem: He had only a short time to find oil before the leases that permitted exploration expired.

In a race against time, Don scurried around to find a reliable company to do drilling in one of the key areas, and he succeeded in getting the drilling started within a week. Sure enough—true to his visions—they struck oil exactly where he had expected. Today, this well alone can yield more than three hundred barrels of oil and some three million cubic feet of gas each day.

But Don hasn't forgotten who it is who has given him the power to acquire his wealth. In one large field as each new well comes in, one third of Don's total interest is given to the Lord's work. With fourteen producing wells, that amounts to $1 million or more each year. And yet Don seldom misses an opportunity to give generously from what remains as his share.

As you can see, Don makes full use of the Law of Reciprocity. He contributes a sizable share of both his business profits and his personal income to God's work. Then, as God has promised, He reciprocates: Don's gifts are miraculously returned to him in new drilling successes.

Still, even with special visions and great material success, it hasn't been easy. "There were many points when I could have gone bankrupt," he recalls. "I'd get in such a bind, I couldn't see any hope of coming out. I'd get out of bed at night and cry out to the Lord, saying, 'Jesus, I need help—there is no way out!' The very next day, after I'd cried out to the Lord, help would always come."

I realize it may be hard to believe that God will reach out and help a person like Don to become very rich, while others are barely eking out a living. But remember: The Lord has different purposes and different gifts for different people. If a person with the talent for finance submits that ability entirely to God's direction, it's likely that amazing things will happen. You might say that Don in effect made God the senior partner in his firm, and God in turn has blessed him financially in miraculous ways.

But not all money miracles involve such huge sums. God may enter the financial side of our lives in a variety of other miraculous ways—as will become evident in the following illustration.

God Never Loses Anything!

Have you ever lost something of value and then found it later under very strange and highly unlikely circumstances?

Bob and Caryl Nejedlo of Green Bay, Wisconsin, had an experience like this. The story begins when Caryl lost a diamond from her ring. She thought it had dropped out when she and her husband were out ice-skating, and she assumed it was irretrievably lost. In fact, she was so sure it was gone that she even had that diamond replaced with another one.

Four years passed, and the Nejedlos, who are dedicated Christians, were trying to make a decision about how much money to give to a Christian ministry. They had been contributing $15 a month to this ministry for a while, but Bob had a sense that they should increase their gift to $1,000. Unfortunately, they didn't have that amount on hand. So where would the extra money come from?

Bob felt that even as they were being told to give more, God would somehow supply the money. He had never had that kind of strong guidance from God's Spirit before about giving to the Lord's work. So he knew if he made the pledge, without having the money on hand, he would be taking a stand on faith—faith that he had heard the divine message correctly and that God would really provide the cash to meet the pledge.

Although Caryl didn't get any message from God as Bob had, she trusted his sensitivity to the Spirit and encouraged him to make the pledge. That's just what he did. And that's when the money miracles began to happen.

The very next night, Bob, Caryl, and their eleven-year-old son, John, were downstairs in their den. Bob tossed a football to his son, and John dropped it. But when John looked down to get the ball, he found something else.

"I saw a glittering object which seemed to be a diamond," he recalls. He picked it up to show his dad, and Bob's immediate response was, "I don't believe it!"

Of course, it was the very diamond that Caryl had lost four years before. To be sure that it was really the same stone, Caryl placed it next to her ring setting. Sure enough, it fit perfectly.

But the Nejedlos grew more incredulous the more they thought about it. Their rug had been cleaned many times during the past four years with a suction cleaner. And about a year before, the carpet had been pulled up from its original location, cut apart, and refitted for a play area of the basement. In fact, the family had almost thrown it out at that time, but they had decided they'd try to get a little more use from it.

Apparently, during this entire period, that diamond had been sitting snugly and safely in that rug, just waiting for God's use. When it was found, the timing was perfect to help the couple meet their pledge. They had it appraised, and the value was estimated to be $750. So they sent it with the appraisal to the ministry to cover three fourths of their $1,000 pledge. But what about the other $250?

Again, God provided. Soon after their amazing discovery of the diamond, Bob and Caryl had to figure out their income taxes, and they discovered they had overpaid their tax and were due a refund. The refund provided the additional $250 they needed to complete their pledge. So in a matter of days, God had miraculously provided $1,000 which allowed them to fulfill their pledge.

Now, some people may think it's stretching a point to believe that finding your own diamond and receiving a refund of your own tax money is some kind of special provision of funds from God. But as with many miracles, we're dealing here with a series of extraordinary happenings which, taken together, become far too unlikely to qualify as mere coincidence.

Remember: The first step in this sequence of events was that the Nejedlos had firmly committed themselves to paying that $1,000 pledge, even if they had to mortgage their family finances in some way to do it. And at the same time, Bob felt that God was telling him that 1) he should give, and 2) provision would be made for the gift. Then, you are confronted with the highly unlikely finding of the lost diamond *and* the discovery of a tax refund, which together just "happen" to add up to the precise amount of the pledge. So in a sense, the family just became a conduit which God could use to further His broader financial purposes in the world through miraculous means.

Of course, unlike Don Dalbosco in the previous example, the Nejedlos didn't get any richer from this miracle. But the benefits that have inured to them are far more valuable than mere money. Caryl says, "Praise God! He has established our faith firmly in His promise, 'Give and He shall give unto you.'"

She indicates that the experience has enormously strengthened the entire family's belief in God's power. Several of their friends and relatives have also come to know God better as a result of hearing about this experience. This particular "miracle over mammon" has been a giant step in one family's understanding of the sovereign control God exercises over our finances.

From Two Dollars to Two Million

Seldom have I encountered a more dramatic story than that of Leon Hooten.

Close your eyes for a minute and visualize a Mid-America success story. Would your vision include a bright, attractive young man who could sell anything? And with that ability, a $15,000 per week personal income, a private airplane, a Mercedes Benz automobile, a twenty-three foot customized motor home, a private mansion? Add a successful automotive dealership, a finance company, and a motor club. And consider business deals waiting to happen that would expand the business empire.

Leon Hooten had all of this until July 1982. With the collapse of Penn Square Bank, the Hooten Automotive Company also collapsed. By May 1983, Leon's $15,000 weekly income, the Mercedes Benz, and every other status symbol that he had so carefully accumulated were gone.

The man who seemed to have a golden touch woke up to the realization that he had lost $300,000 personally and his business had lost $750,000. His total wealth consisted of two dollars in cash and a shotgun.

Unable to stand the shame and humiliation of failure, Leon went upstairs to his bedroom. In the corner of the room was his shotgun and what seemed to him the only way out. He sat on the edge of the bed, fingering the cold steel of the weapon. Then, for some reason, he flicked on the television set in the bedroom. Was it one last dose of escapism? Or was it to drown out the noise of the gun blast?

But the shotgun blast was never heard because God had other plans for Leon Hooten. The image on the screen was my associate, Ben Kinchlow, a tall, striking-looking black man, urging the viewers to give their burdens to Jesus Christ. As Ben invited the viewers to pray with him, Leon Hooten quietly laid the shotgun on the floor and gave his life, his shame, and his financial problems to Jesus Christ.

Then in a burst of generosity, he called our counseling center, and like the widow in Jesus' day, gave God all he had. Leon pledged his last two dollars to help us help others. In his words, "Then I didn't have a meal for the night."

But a great peace flooded his life. He knew everything would be all right.

But Leon could not have dreamed how fast it would happen. Before that evening was over, the telephone rang. At the other end of the line was a friend who said, "Leon, I have some money for you." In fact, it was quite a bit of money—enough to pay Leon's pressing bills and feed his family.

And shortly after that, a friend called to say that he had an idea for a business and wanted Leon to be a part of it.

That one idea was so powerful that within one year, Leon Hooten had not only recovered financially but had accumulated an ownership position in a new company worth an estimated $2.5 million. The idea—a prepaid dental and medical-insurance program—was first called Dental Plan of Oklahoma, and now has been renamed Dental Plan of America. On the first anniversary of Leon's total surrender of himself and his last two dollars to Jesus Christ, his new company had twelve-hundred independent sales agents, a home office staff of twenty-five, and policyholders in all fifty states as well as in Ireland, Japan, and Australia. The company is moving into its own building in Oklahoma City with state-of-the-art automation and computerized facilities.

As Leon Hooten puts it, "Dental Plan of America is a debt-free business that operates on the principles of God's Kingdom. It is a showplace of Christian business principles."

But what about Leon Hooten's personal life? He and his business give a tithe of their income to God's work. Leon no longer needs the status symbols of worldly success. Even though his share in the business makes him a millionaire, he lives six blocks from the office building. He says simply, "I have it all—salvation, the Lord, my life, my family. I need no more."

It's clear to me that God can do miraculous things with our money, our personal budgets, and our investments if only we'll give Him half a chance. Many times, He may choose simultaneously to work some incredible physical, emotional, or spiritual transformation, even as He helps in a material way. That's because He is interested in us as total human beings—not just creatures with financial needs.

CHAPTER EIGHT

The Master Keys to Miracles

A few years back, a black gospel singer from Pittsburgh named Danniebelle Hall made famous a song entitled "Ordinary People." Indeed, the stories told in this book deal with ordinary people who at a moment in twentieth-century America encountered the power of an extraordinary God. The God of the Bible, the God of Abraham, the God of Moses, the God of David, the God of Jesus, the God of Peter and Paul.

And in the twentieth century—full of scientific marvels and profound skepticism—simple faith in the God of the Bible did what science, reason, and logic could not do. It brought about miracles for ordinary people just like you and me.

As we reflect on Kathy Kovacs, healed of disfiguring lupus; or Kirt Hadick dramatically healed of cancer; or Janice Gravely spared supernaturally from sure death in an airplane crash; or Don Dalbosco given unusual revelations to locate oil, we soon realize that there is not a tidy little formula to guarantee miracles. God is infinite, and there is no way that our finite minds will ever understand all there is to know about Him of whom the Apostle Paul declared, "His ways are past finding out." His power is only partially understood by our spirits and is truly "beyond reason."

Yet Jesus Christ told his disciples, "The works that I do, you shall do. And greater works than these because I go to my Father." He told all who would follow Him, "Whatsoever you ask the Father in my name, that will I do, that the Father may be glorified in the Son." "Greater works" than Jesus Himself performed and "whatsoever we ask." This mandate of authority is awesome, and would be a cruel hoax unless it were true and understandably attainable.

So in summary, we ask again what is required to enter the invisible realm of unlimited possibility called the Kingdom of God? And what can ordinary people do to bring the miracle power of God's Kingdom into the day-to-day world where we live? Certain things stand out.

A New Reflecting Mirror

First, we must recognize that there is a ladder of power and authority. It flows from God's Spirit to man's spirit, to man's soul or mind, to his body, and out to the material world. Most people have the ladder of power reversed. They are manipulated by the material world, which dominates their bodies and minds, which in turn suppress their spirits, while they ignore or reject God's Spirit.

According to the theologians, this happens because of a problem called "original sin." Here's how it came about.

At creation, our first ancestor, Adam, was given a perfect spirit. Adam's spirit was similar to the giant reflecting mirrors in today's high-powered telescopes. These mirrors reflect and magnify the image of far-distant stars and galaxies. Even so, Adam's spirit reflected and magnified the image of God. To Adam, it was easy to understand the ladder of power, because the highest source of power—God Himself—was the most brilliant image at the center of his very being. Other things were in proper perspective because they paled into insignificance when compared to the Glory of God.

But Adam chose to disobey God. He did the one and only thing that he had been told not to do. With that act of disobedience and rebellion, Adam's spirit became damaged. It was as if the giant reflecting mirror within him that was capable of seeing God had been struck by a stone and shattered. What is called the *imago dei*, the image of God, within him was obscured. He could no longer see God or His Kingdom clearly. Now he had to depend on his reason, his senses, his body, his mind, the world around him. What mattered was staying alive—earning a living—surviving in the jungle. Instead of a being dedicated to bring glory to God, there came to be a creature with Godlike attributes, dedicated to self-preservation. Therefore, it should come as no surprise to learn that, only a few generations after Adam, the "world was filled with violence," and "every imagination of man was on evil continually."

It is this condition—a sort of moral handicap—that is called original sin. You and I were born with it. In fact, everybody in the world suffers from it at birth. The only solution offered by the Bible is a "second birth." In fact, Jesus Christ told one of the religious leaders of his day—an exemplary man by human standards—that unless he was "born again," he could neither see the Kingdom of God nor enter it. There must be a time when God's Spirit remakes our spirit—our inner spiritual mirror—so that His Spirit and His image within us shine brightly again, and in turn become the central motivating force of our being.

This is a profound miracle, but is accomplished by five simple steps. One, admit that you have done things that are wrong in God's sight, and that you, not God, have been in charge of your life. Two, turn away from selfishness, sin, and disobedience. Three, accept the fact that Jesus Christ died to pay the penalty required for your sins. Accept Him as your Savior. Four, open your heart (your spirit) to Jesus Christ. Invite Him to join His Spirit with your spirit. Make Him from that moment on the undisputed Lord of your life. Five, believe that you have accomplished what is required to be born again, and thank God privately and publicly for what He has done for you.

The one who is born again begins to see the Kingdom of God. The Bible comes alive. The reality of spiritual things bursts again and again upon the consciousness. This person is inner-directed by God's Spirit joined with his own spirit. Vistas of spiritual opportunity stretch out before him. The ladder of power has been established properly. Yet there is much, much more.

The Power of Authority and Exploding Power

"The Greeks," it is said, "had a word for it." Indeed they did. They seemed to have precise words for everything. In English we use the word *power* to cover many situations. But in the Greek language of the New Testament, there were two words for power—each conveying significantly different meanings. One word is *exousia*. It conveys the power of authority that a king or president or God Himself might have by virtue of his position. The President of the United States could be a ninety-pound weakling. Yet by virtue of his *exousia* over the U.S. nuclear arsenal, he can incinerate entire cities. Jesus referred to His own mandate of authority when He declared, "All *exousia* in heaven and in earth is given to me; go ye therefore . . ." (Matthew 28:18–19)

Jesus Himself has the power by virtue of a grant of authority from God the Father over every government, principality, or hierarchy on this earth or in the spiritual kingdom. There is no authority—other than that of the Father—that surpasses or supersedes the authority given to Jesus.

In what is called "the great commission," Jesus clearly extends a grant of authority to His followers. This authority encompasses the spread of His Kingdom, the spread of His teaching, and of His authority to all the nations of the world. To put it another way, Christian believers have been deputized by Jesus Christ for the purpose of gathering subjects for His Kingdom. Pursuant to this commission, they have authority over Satan, his angels, and any other force of authority that opposes the lordship of Christ.

Luke, in his Gospel, tells us that Jesus made the grant of *exousia* even more explicit. In Luke 10:19, we read, "Behold, I give you the power [authority] to trample on serpents and scorpions, and over all the power of the enemy." Here we see not only clear authority over Satan and whatever came from him, but the restoration of the authority over the serpent, which Adam lost in the Garden of Eden.

Jesus gave to his disciples further extensions of His own *exousia* when He told them to pray "in His name." We read, "And whatsoever you will ask in my name, that will I do. . . . If you ask anything in my name, I will do it." (John 14:13, 14) This grant of authority resembles a modern-day power of attorney by which one person permits a trusted friend or adviser to sign papers disposing of money or property as if it were his.

Therefore, we see that the ability to perform miracles rests not only on a relationship to Jesus Christ as Savior and Lord, but also on an understanding of the clear and sweeping grant of authority given to His people to act in His name. The bold faith that will experience extraordinary miracles must have its firm foundation in biblical privileges. You will not see miraculous things happen unless you believe they can and should happen. And, normally speaking, you will not believe unless you are familiar with the privileges given to you by the Lord in the Bible. "Faith," wrote the Apostle Paul, "cometh by hearing, and hearing by the Word of God." (Romans 10:17)

There is no substitute for careful and prayerful study of God's promises—until they, like God Himself, become the central reality of your life.

The second New Testament Greek word that we translate "power" is *dunamis*. *Dunamis* carried the concept of resident strength or explosive force. The English word *dynamite* comes from *dunamis*.

A U.S. President has *exousia* over the nuclear arsenal. The atomic bombs in the arsenal have *dunamis*.

Before He ascended to heaven after His resurrection, Jesus commanded His followers not to leave Jerusalem until they received *dunamis*. He told them, "You shall receive *dunamis* when the Holy Spirit has come upon you, and you shall be witnesses unto me. . . ." (Acts 1:8) This outpouring of explosive power would come about through an experience that Jesus described as being "baptized with the Holy Spirit."

Surely then, this extraordinary experience is connected to miracles, to the ladder of power, to energizing the human words that still storms, heal the sick, cast out demons, and proclaim the truth of the Kingdom of God.

Indeed we see that the Apostle Paul in his first letter to the Corinthians mentions nine manifestations (or gifts) of the Holy Spirit—among them gifts of healing, the manifestation of supernatural faith, and the working of miracles.

How then do you receive this energizing power? The Bible suggests five steps:

1. *Ask for it.* Jesus said, "Ask and you shall receive."
2. *Be prepared to obey the Holy Spirit.* The Apostle Peter told an assembled crowd in Jerusalem that the Holy Spirit was given to them that obey Him.
3. *Offer your body to God.* The Apostle Paul, writing to the church at Rome, commanded the people to "present your bodies, a living sacrifice, holy, acceptable to God, which is your reasonable service." (Romans 12:1) Miracle power and the Holy Spirit do not live comfortably with unsurrendered flesh. Those who are gluttons, drunkards, sensual, selfish, and greedy will not know God's great power. God's best requires a new man. The Holy Spirit gives life; our old life stinks of death.
4. *Receive by faith.* The Apostle Paul asked the Galatian church, "Did you receive the Holy Spirit by the works of the law or the hearing of faith?" (Galatians 3:2) The power of the Holy Spirit, like every other good thing from God, comes to us by simple faith. We do not earn a place in the family of God. We do not earn miracles. We do not earn the power of God's Spirit. They come through faith because of undeserved favor from God.
5. *Act your faith.* In the New Testament, the natural consequence of baptism with power was an expression of prayer or praise in a language unknown to the

speaker. This wonderful expression of glossalalia or tongues was the sure sign that a person's speech had been energized by God. God's Spirit was directing the human speech, and obvious power was being released to the world.

Mere human words become instruments of divine power for healing, for the prayer of faith, for casting out demons, for rebuking a killer hurricane or a killer frost. The same God who brought the universe into being by a spoken word by the Baptism with the Holy Spirit will make your words like His. Experience the adventure of demonstrating the *dunamis* that He gives to you.

Perseverance

During the years that I have served Jesus, it has been my privilege to see a number of instantaneous miracles. I prayed for a woman in Calgary, Alberta, Canada, who had been deaf in one ear for fifty years. Her deaf ear opened instantly and she could hear perfectly. At a gathering of youth in Front Royal, Virginia, a man suffering with multiple sclerosis was present in a wheelchair. After prayer, he got out of the wheelchair and walked from the meeting, pushing the chair ahead of him. In Virginia Beach, just recently, a couple brought a young child who was so crippled by arthritis that she could not run or walk properly. That afternoon, after a simple prayer, the child was running up and down stairs with no effects whatsoever of her disease.

Each year through my *700 Club* television program, I see or hear about some fifty thousand people who have received miraculous answers to prayer—most of them instantaneous. Tumors and cysts disappear, cancer is healed, disfiguring scars vanish, twisted limbs straighten, retarded children develop mental acuity, diseased organs become normal, marriages are restored, miracles of finance take place.

Yet God's normal order is not instantaneous. He normally gives to those who persevere. Many times there are attitudes that need changing. Many times there must be a surrender of deliberate disobedience to God's commands. Many times there is self-pity; and in some cases, there is a will to be sick. As we pray in a determined fashion, we change. We grow more yielded to God, more willing to obey Him, more ready to rid our lives of spiritual hindrances.

Prayer does not change God; it changes us. His will is always benevolent. But He would be sending us the wrong signal if He permitted miraculous blessings while we were going against His will for our lives.

So Jesus tells us: Keep on asking and you will receive. Keep on seeking, and you will find. Keep on knocking and the door will be opened.

Knowing How

Although I have stated repeatedly that there is no simple formula that brings about a miracle, nevertheless, there are certain elements that need to be understood.

1. Prayer Prayer can be silent or spoken. Simple or flowery. By rote or extemporaneous. But to be effective, prayer must be spiritual communion between two spirits. As the Psalmist put it, "Deep calls unto deep." Deep within your being there must be communion with your creator. You speak to Him, but mainly He should speak to you.

171

Great prayer—miracle prayer—is not so much a matter of asking but listening. What is God's will in the matter? What does He intend to do? When does He intend to do it?

One incident stands out. In 1958 when I was serving as the student assistant pastor of a stately old church in Mt. Vernon, New York, I took the young people of the church for an ice-skating party at Bear Mountain Lake in the Catskills. One lovely little twelve-year-old girl lives in my memory. She was sweet, animated, and full of life. I had learned that she was an orphan and was not surprised on that crisp, sun-drenched Saturday afternoon to find her showing the same affection toward my wife and me that we experienced from our own children.

The next day she and a girl friend were in church. After the service, they skipped down the front steps of the Gothic structure. And without pausing to look, they both ran in front of an approaching sedan. The friend was hurled in the air and landed in a sitting position, bruised but without serious injury, about twenty feet in front of the car.

My little orphan friend was not so fortunate. The bumper of the car struck her with full force right at her knees. The angle of the blow caused her head to whip back with a sickening thud into the hood of the sedan. She slid off and fell to the ground unconscious.

An ambulance rushed her to the hospital. My friend Harald Bredesen and I followed close behind. I was sick with grief at the tragedy I had just witnessed. Yet I was determined that my little friend was not going to die.

We waited nervously in one of those drab hospital waiting rooms. Finally a grim-faced surgeon appeared. "Reverend," he said, "half of her brain has turned to jelly. If she lives, she will be a vegetable." I pressed him for hope. He could give little. Then we told him, "We are asking God for a miracle. It's going to happen. Please keep working with her." His face filled with understanding and compassion. Promising to keep trying, he left us.

This scene kept repeating itself for the next five hours. The men of God grasping for a miracle. The man of medicine watching a child die, but hoping within himself for the miracle to happen.

Sometime within that long vigil, I asked God for a word of encouragement. Reaching my hand into my breast pocket, I slipped out a red-letter New Testament. Here is what my eye saw: "Blessed are they that die in the Lord from henceforth." (Revelation 14:13)

God was telling me that this little child, whose mother and father were both dead, did not have a very promising future on earth. Her destiny and her happiness lay with Him in heaven.

I quietly closed the little New Testament and slipped it back in my pocket. Then I said to myself, "I must be mistaken. God is not going to let that child die."

Then we really began to pray. We spoke divine healing over the unconscious child. We anointed her with oil. We rebuked the death angel and forbade him to take her. We called upon the Lord with all the faith we could muster.

About six o'clock that evening, the child died.

But we weren't finished. We continued to pray.

The mortician came and took away her body. After he had embalmed it, he placed her in an open casket in the church on Monday evening.

We refused to accept what had happened and went into the church to pray that the child would rise from the dead.

She did not rise and we buried her on Tuesday.

God had clearly shown me from Scripture that from His perspective, the little child was happier being in heaven than she would have been had she stayed on earth. My prayer should have been ended when I learned God's will. How much needless anguish I would have been spared had I accepted His clear answer to me.

In this case, the answer was no. Usually the answer is yes. Sometimes the answer is "not yet." At other times, it is "There needs to be a change."

Obviously, we can ask God for what we want. But better still that we should ask God to show us what He wants.

2. A Command with Authority Once we are clear that God wills a thing, we can ask Him for it. But having asked, we then should command it to be done in Jesus' name. Remember the ladder of authority. Power flows from God's spirit to our spirit to our mind to our mouth to the material world around us.

In the name of Jesus, we command demons to come out and they obey us. We command cancer to leave and it departs. We command healing to take place and cells are healed. And on at least three recorded occasions, we learn that Jesus Christ commanded the dead to rise and they obeyed Him.

3. Remove the Chief Hindrance Your personal ability to experience miracles depends on a relationship with God as His child, a grant of His authority, and the empowering of His Holy Spirit. All of these things depend on God's willingness to forgive your sins, which in turn enables you to see the secret world of spiritual power and to enter it.

But one thing will cut off your vision of the invisible kingdom and will nullify your access to God's power. That one thing is lack of forgiveness. Jesus Christ put it this way, "And whenever you stand praying, forgive if you have anything against anyone; so that your Father also who is in Heaven may forgive you your trespasses." (Matthew 6:14)

If you hold a grudge against an enemy, a friend, an employee, your husband, your wife, your son, your daughter, a

174

brother, a sister, yourself, or God, you will never see miracles happen in your life. Regardless of legal right or wrong, regardless of how justified you may be, regardless of what others tell you, you must forgive. And the forgiveness must be deep, sincere, thorough. You must forgive the other person. You must ask God to forgive you for your attitude; then you must begin actively to pray that God will bless the person who has wronged you.

In this regard, I am reminded of a girl named Gwen Burke who had contracted polio when she was only fourteen months old. She had to learn to walk with a brace, and she endured callous remarks and jokes about her handicap throughout high school and into her adult life.

"When I reached high school, our entire school life revolved around school dances," she recalled. "That was probably one of the biggest hurts in my life—sitting at those dances, all dolled up, in a pretty dress, waiting for a guy to ask me to dance. But it just couldn't happen."

As the hurts cut deeper and deeper, Gwen began to blame God for her problem. "I wanted to be healed. I used to go and sit at the back of the church and as I waited for my mother to pick me up from school, I'd pray that God would let me walk down the aisle. So I not only became bitter about myself, but I became bitter that God wouldn't do something for me."

Later, even though she married a wonderful man named Bill, this bitterness caused Gwen to plunge into a deep depression. She isolated herself in the house, and refused to go out. She had started a dog-grooming business but would deal only with customers who would bring their dogs to her home and leave them there.

But then one customer, a woman who was determined to bring Gwen out of her shell, insisted that Gwen make a house call to groom her dog. During the evening's work, the woman told Gwen that she was wrong to sit around feeling sorry for herself. One thing led to another, until finally, at this woman's suggestion, Gwen prayed to ask Jesus Christ to take control of her life.

The change in Gwen was dramatic. She started attending church, and her musical talents blossomed as she sang of what God had done for her. Finally, the healing that she had prayed for so long began to occur. It started during a visit to the church by a speaker who told her to go home and take off her brace.

"Generally, when I would take the brace off, the sciatic nerve would just go crazy," she said. "I would end up in a pile on the floor somewhere. [But this time] that didn't happen."

The muscles that were supposed to have atrophied beyond repair began to grow, and the healing has been steady ever since this experience. What is especially interesting about Gwen's story is that the first thing she had to get over was that feeling of self-pity—the feeling that God had abandoned her. She had blamed God, and then realizing she was wrong, she in effect "forgave" God and sought his forgiveness at the same time.

If you have a grudge against somebody who has hurt you— or who you *think* has hurt you—you probably won't experience a miracle. The miracle you look for depends on your being in a state of forgiveness. When Gwen entered into that state of forgiveness, great reservoirs of supernatural power were released in her.

A Future Filled with Hope

It has been said that the past is prologue. And indeed the miraculous accounts in this book can be the prologue—the introductory scene—to a future of hope and power for each one who reads it.

THE MASTER KEYS TO MIRACLES

The age of miracles is not past. In fact, many believe that we are standing on the threshold of a visitation from God upon our world of such power that seemingly incredible miracles will then seem commonplace.

I have related for you actual accounts of extraordinary physical and mental healings and the demonstration of God's power over nature and finances. But these true-life stories from our twentieth century are just a tiny part of the millions of miracles that are taking place in the lives of ordinary people around the world today.

You can experience God's miracle power to help you recover from disease, to see a stormy marriage restored, to be freed from mental fear and bondage, to overcome financial hardships, to find protection against the awesome force of natural disaster, and to live confidently, victoriously, and above the circumstances and tragedies of your life.

Entrance into the Kingdom of God—the secret kingdom, the world of miracles, the miracle dimension—must be with knowledge of and submission to God's will and plan for you. In summary, I suggest these simple steps to enable you to experience the miraculous in your life:

- You must be spiritually reborn.
- You must rely on the biblical mandate of authority.
- You must be baptized in the Holy Spirit.
- You must be willing to persevere in faith.
- You must know how to pray.
- You must declare the will of God with authority.
- You must forgive if you have aught against anyone.

Above all else, you must make the supreme quest of your life knowing and loving the eternal God who is the creator of all, and our loving, heavenly father.

BEYOND REASON

The reservoirs of supernatural power are open to you and me. To ordinary people everywhere. To a new race of redeemed people who can bring the love of God to bear to alleviate suffering and sickness and poverty and despair. To people who indeed have learned to live a life that is BEYOND REASON.